KT-447-632

Slow at Work

Slow at Work

How to work less, achieve more
and regain your balance in
an always-on world

Aoife McElwain

Gill Books

Gill Books
Hume Avenue
Park West
Dublin 12
www.gillbooks.ie

Gill Books is an imprint of M.H. Gill & Co.

© Aoife McElwain 2017
978 07171 7357 0

Print origination by O'K Graphic Design, Dublin
Copy-edited by Matthew Parkinson-Bennett
Proofread by Jane Rogers
Printed by ScandBook AB, Sweden

This book is typeset in 10/16 pt Formata with headings in Neutra Text sBook

The paper used in this book comes from the wood pulp of managed forests.
For every tree felled, at least one tree is planted, thereby renewing natural
resources.

All rights reserved.
No part of this publication may be copied, reproduced or transmitted in any
form or by any means without written permission of the publishers.

A CIP catalogue record for this book is available from the British Library.

5 4 3 2

*For Eugene and Pauline, who gave me
the gift of grit.*

Aoife McElwain is a food writer and creative events planner.
She writes about food for *The Irish Times* and *Totally Dublin*.
She is one half of the video and recipe series *forkful.tv* and
works as a food stylist across print, digital and TV. She is the
Programme Curator and Community Manager of Turkfest,
a community-led arts and music festival on a small island
called Inishturk, home to just 58 people, off the west coast
of Ireland. She is host of the Sing Along Social, a zero-
commitment choir that brings friends and strangers together
to sing along to their favourite tunes. She is the founder and
curator of the slow:series, a talk series delving into different
aspects of the slow movement.

Contents

Banana-level Busyness

A MOMENT OF BANANA CLARITY

I'm sitting at my desk, working on one of the multitude of projects that I'm juggling. I'm firefighting emails about an event that I'm producing in a few days. I have about 20 tabs open on my browser, trying to finish some research on a food article that's due to be with my editor at *The Irish Times* in the next 40 minutes. Meanwhile, I'm also trying to confirm dates for a food photography shoot for a client.

'Will you have that piece for me soon?' pings an email message from my ever-patient editor, the notification shooting out from my phone like an anxiety bullet. *Why didn't you just get up earlier yesterday and finish that piece before you started this other work?* says my Inner Critic. *Typical*, my Inner Critic continues. *You're just not working hard enough.*

Leabharlanna Poibli Chathair Baile Átha Cliath
Dublin City Public Libraries

My phone has been noisily vibrating on the table next to my laptop, pinging with tweets, Instagram and Facebook notifications, screaming for my attention. 'Look at me! Hey! Hey! HEYYYYYY!' they screech, in a cacophony of technological noise. Back on my laptop, I try to finish one of the three email replies that I'm currently working on. Then PING! another email notification comes through, so I pick up my phone and start replying to that email while the ones on my laptop get left behind.

Throughout all of this, a crescendo of panic has been rising from my belly up into my chest, as my mind goes into overdrive trying to manage the deadlines, ideas, fears and tasks buzzing around my brain, competing for attention in a web of chaos. I've been up since 6am and I haven't eaten a proper breakfast yet (who has time for breakfast, anyway? Certainly not people who write about food for a living) but I *have* had three coffees and it's only 10.30 am.

And suddenly I have a moment of clarity: This way of working is totally bananas. Like, completely crazy.

I stop everything that I'm doing and think, very clearly, 'I have *got* to figure out a better way of working.'

▶-◇-◀

Hi. My name is Aoife. I'm a freelance food writer, food stylist, creative events planner and treasure hunt enthusiast. Welcome to *Slow at Work*, my personal management plan of how to slow down at work and still keep up. Since my epiphany back in November 2015, I have been committed to figuring out whether it's possible to slow down at work and still keep up. Part of that process has been working on this book.

I'm guessing you've had similar days of banana-level busyness, where you're more flustered than productive, more frazzled than on it. Contrary to the utopian ideals put forward in the last century of a four-hour work day or even a four-*day* work week, we seem to be working more, and we appear to be experiencing more stress, anxiety and depression too.[1]

A YouGov survey commissioned by Virgin in 2015 found that 51% of full-time UK employees have experienced anxiety or burnout in their jobs.[2] The National Study of Wellbeing of Hospital Doctors in Ireland conducted research in 2017 and found that one in three doctors working in Ireland have experienced burnout.[3] In an article for the *Harvard Business Review*, Emma Seppala and Marissa King compared results of the 2016 General Social Survey with results from about 20 years before. They found that people in 2016 were 'twice as likely to report that they are always exhausted. Close to

3

50% of people say they are often or always exhausted due to work.'[4]

It might feel like we are experiencing an acceleration of speed, pace and responsibility in the workplace, but to experience exhaustion actually isn't anything new. In an *Irish Times* magazine article encompassing a brief history of burnout, writer Patrick Freyne referenced the book *Exhaustion: A History* by Anna Katharina Schaffner.[5] What we call burnout was once known as neurasthenia, a trendy diagnosis for the creative crowd of the 19th century, among them Virginia Woolf and Franz Kafka.

Shaffner argues that to experience exhaustion or burnout isn't something unique to our era. 'The ancient Greeks were very concerned about the waning of our energies,' she writes. 'In the 18th century people were talking about an exhaustion epidemic. In the 19th century they thought they'd reached a pinnacle of exhaustion that they had never reached before … what changes is the way we theorise exhaustion and the narratives we tell about its causes.'

One of the first and best books I read in my exploration of slowness was *In Praise of Slow* by the Canadian journalist and writer Carl Honoré. This bestselling book was first published in 2004, three whole years before the iPhone was released.

These days, Honoré's work still revolves around promoting his idea of 'less frantic, more flow'. I reached out to this slow productivity expert to see what changes he had seen in the last decade and a half. Was work actually getting faster?

'I think one thing that has changed enormously since 2004 is the movement of information,' Honoré tells me over Skype from his London home. 'We live in a maelstrom of data and distraction. That gives us the impression that everything is going faster and I think that part of the problem is that we have swallowed whole the idea that everything is getting faster and therefore we have to get faster, too.'

We seem to have a perception problem. We have embraced the notion that no humans have ever felt this time poor. Yet research continues to indicate that we actually have more leisure time than ever.[6] In 2015 the global marketing firm Havas Worldwide conducted a survey of ten thousand adults of different ages in 28 countries. Their survey respondents appeared to show an interesting trend suggesting that people tend to pretend to be busier than they actually are.[7]

Whether or not we are The Busiest or The Most Stressed workers of all time is beside the point. It is apparent that for many people, even the most beloved of jobs can easily shift towards being a severe source of burnout and toxic stress rather than the fulfilling, challenging and purpose-filled work we crave.

Work can become a happiness inhibitor and an exhaustive strain on our natural resources of creativity, talent and skills. When this happens, we simply aren't firing on all cylinders and our capacity for productivity is not at its best. That has been true for me, and if you're reading this book it's likely it's been true for you, too.

From activists, farmers, doctors, politicians, designers and musicians, pretty much everyone I interviewed for this book had, to varying degrees, felt the sting of burnout at some point in their careers.

Well, except for maybe The Venerable Panchen Ötrul Rinpoche, a Buddhist monk I met who lives in Cavan. He was super chill.

What are we doing to ourselves and does it have to be this way? Is burnout inevitable? Can we escape the cult of busyness? Is it possible to slow down and still keep up?

WHY SLOW DOWN?

I learned how to drive in 2016 and my driving instructor, Leah Cullen, was a bit of a zen master. On one of my first driving lessons, she said to me: 'The road is like life. It's just going to keep throwing stressful shit at you and your job is to get through it as calmly as possible.' That kind of sums up the slow approach I'm looking for at work and in life.

That approach does not come naturally to me. I am not a zen master. But boy do I love a project.

In my working life, I've worked as a project manager in a creative strategy and design company – facilitating workshops, curating events and connecting creative entrepreneurs to resources and communities. I've taught English as a second language to people from all over the world in Dublin and to Saudi women in Saudi Arabia. I've worked in a crèche. I've led 2,000 people in a singalong to the Backstreet Boys at Body & Soul festival as part of my Sing Along Social project. I've been a waitress in Dublin, London and New York. I've interviewed Bill Murray on the red carpet at SXSW in Austin, Texas for an online documentary. I've made 16 consecutive bowls of porridge look pretty (and identical) for a TV commercial for a leading supermarket. I've project managed fundraising events. I've been an Airbnb host. I've worked on arts and cultural events around Ireland, including an island party for 150 people on Inishturk off the coast of Mayo, home ordinarily to just 58 people. I once managed a Twitter account for a famous person's dog. My career has been unstrategic, varied and rich.

Currently I work for myself as a freelance food writer, food stylist and creative events planner. I write regular columns and features for *The Irish Times* and *Totally Dublin* magazine. I started a food blog in 2009 and in 2012 co-founded a video website called *forkful*. I work as a recipe developer and food stylist for brands, helping them to develop recipes and make their food look pretty for social media, print and TV commercials. I run a monthly event called the Sing Along Social, a zero-commitment choir designed for people who can't sing. I get a bunch of people together, pick an artist or a theme, press play and let everyone sing along. I've brought the event to major music and arts festivals, as well as touring it around Ireland, bringing the craic to public and private events. What started as pure fun has turned into a proper job.

I'm a person who loves to work so much and whose identity is so closely linked to my achievements at work that I have regularly put my mental health under tremendous pressure. I've gotten so wrapped up in projects that I valued their success over my own needs or the needs of those closest to me. Over the last couple of years, I had started to feel like I was stuck in a cycle of extreme activity followed by exhausted burnout. Project after project, deadline after deadline, task after task, mixed in with plenty of meltdowns, self-doubt and fear made for a cocktail of dread, fatigue and depression. Even though I was carving out my own tailor-made career and doing the things I loved ... well, I wasn't loving it.

My trouble with work really became a serious problem when I went freelance early in the summer of 2015. I thought that by going freelance I'd finally be in control of my time. I'd be able to manage things in a more sustainable way, and not be trying to pursue my extra-curricular activities like blogging and event planning while holding down a totally separate full-time job.

Pretty soon, I discovered a terrible truth: I was the worst boss I'd ever had. I didn't care about my employee's wellbeing. Like, *at all*. I made her work at all times of the day, night and weekend. I had no boundaries. I woke her up in the middle of the night to tell her what a shitty job she was doing.

I also didn't care about my employee's physical health. Eventually, after three years of lugging around crates full of plates, crockery, cups, pots and pans when working on photography shoots as a food stylist, my back finally said 'I'm out of here.' A slipped disc and a nasty bout of sciatica meant nearly a year of intensive physiotherapy from summer 2015 to summer 2016. This back injury also meant I had absolutely no choice but to slow down at work. It's a cliché, but it was a blessing in disguise. I was forced into rethinking how I was approaching life and work.

Because I'm a compulsively busy person, when I had my moment of clarity and realised I needed to rethink work and figure out how to slow down, I immediately (and I mean *immediately*), in the midst of all those deadlines and tasks, started to put in motion what would become the slow:series. This was a series of talks and workshops I put together throughout 2016 to look at slowing down at work, which in turn led to the opportunity to write this book. So, my way of slowing down was to do *more* ... you can see the commitment to over-working that I'm dealing with here, right?

WHO IS THIS BOOK FOR AND HOW DOES IT WORK?

This book is for people who love their work but who might be struggling in their search for the elusive work–life balance. Those who feel trapped in a cult of busyness, slaves to speed and under the control of a relentless pace of life and work. It's for those who have established themselves in their chosen field but are questioning their ability to keep up with the sprint of success. It's for workers starting out on their career paths who want to figure out the best way to manage their energy in the long term.

In order to maintain consistent productivity at work, I have realised I need to cultivate a sustainable, and therefore slower, approach to work. To figure out how to do that I wanted to take a closer look at the areas that were causing me trouble and see if by examining them at a deeper level, I might be able to change the way I was working. Areas like procrastination, boundaries and learning to say no. Would it be possible for me to tame my Inner Critic? I wanted to take a long hard look at how I was using technology. Was it healthy? Was it useful, even? Could I learn to manage my energy so that I could be more productive at work?

The stories shared by the people I've spoken to in this book provide another perspective outside the cult of busyness, or perhaps just on the edge, to explore how they have approached work and slowing down, so that you can figure out whether that's an option for you. In these pages, you'll find out what I have read, heard and learned since that epiphany in November 2015.

As I am not a productivity expert, an organisational psychologist or a life coach, I sought out experts in my quest to improve my own relationship with work. I reached out to People Who Know About These Kinds of Things. I talked to work coaches, organisational psychologists, chief happiness officers and mindfulness teachers from around Ireland and the world. I read books, essays, articles and research papers about procrastination, changing mindsets, self-compassion and grit, selecting quotes that I found to be personally useful to share with you in these pages.

To find inspiration I also spoke to a wide range of workers from Ireland and around the world, from farmers to comedians, teachers to activists, lawyers to writers, about how they support themselves at work. The stories and wisdom I picked up along the way is what you'll find in these pages.

Isn't it funny/annoying how we can keep learning the same lesson over and over again until it finally sinks in? At the end of each chapter, I've put together 'Five Slow Notes to Self'. These are the key learnings that I've taken from each chapter. I've pulled them out to remind myself of the lessons I've learned – and my hope is that you can find some learning in these lessons, too. They are my goals and what I think are important ingredients in creating a more sustainable work–life balance for myself, and they might give you some food for thought, too. I've also included a reading list at the end of each chapter to give you some jumping off points for further research.

This book revolves around the privilege of choice. It's a privilege to work hard in a job you love. Not everyone is afforded the same luxury. There are those whose place of birth or socio-economic background simply doesn't offer them the same opportunities as those born into a different set of circumstances. The topic of slowing down could be seen as one giant first world problem. Pretty much everyone I spoke to for this book checked their privilege at the beginning of our conversation.

Part of the problem is that in the upbringing and culture many of us share, the word 'slow' itself has negative connotations and an association with laziness. I'd like to challenge that perception. I don't want to be ashamed of admitting that the pace I felt was expected of me isn't what I want for my life.

I'm grateful to be busy at work, that's a given. But it's dangerous not to allow yourself to accept that you're struggling because you don't want to seem ungrateful about the opportunities you've been given. It can also be possible to want to change our relationship with work while feeling grateful for having work in the first place.

Writing a book was perhaps an extreme way to go about figuring out how to slow down at work. It has certainly been a very meta project. I totally procrastinated on the procrastination chapter and felt like a *complete* imposter while writing the imposter chapter. But, wow, what an opportunity to take a look at the way I've been working and figure out how to work in a way that's more sustainable.

For me, slow means calm and considered yet flexible and fluid – anything too rigid is the enemy of slow. It definitely doesn't mean coming to a complete stop. It means stepping outside the cult of busyness to gain some perspective on the way we are choosing to spend our work days and consider whether we have the power to change how we work to make it more sustainable for ourselves. Whether we can learn skills to catch the rising panic before it takes over our work day. Whether we can slow down at work and still keep up. I hope what I've learned and what I continue to learn serves as a source of learning for you too.

PART ONE

INSIDE

ONE

Procrastination

A pretty foolproof way to recognise when you're procrastinating is finding yourself Googling the word 'procrastination'.

The *Oxford English Dictionary* defines procrastination, quite simply, as the action of delaying or postponing something. But if you're a procrastinator you'll know that there's a whole heap more to it. It's not just a simple case of bad time management. The consequences of procrastination are glaringly obvious (missing deadlines, annoying co-workers, losing your job, never achieving your goals ...), yet it appears to be a frustratingly compelling state to be in. If the results of procrastination are so clear, why do we still do it on repeat?

If you've ever procrastinated (and it's *very* likely you have – heck, maybe you're procrastinating *right now*), you're in good company. Great company, actually. In 2014, the prolific Canadian author Margaret Atwood tweeted to herself, and the world, the following: 'Okay. Enough procrastination. Into the Writing Burrow! In! In! Or no doggie treat + catnip mouse for YOU.'[8] Douglas Adams, author of *The Hitchhiker's Guide to The Galaxy*, famously said: 'I love deadlines. I love the whooshing noise they make as they go by.'[9]

Procrastination can bring with it a particularly sharp level of self-loathing. '*Why* am I watching this video of a man chasing a bat around his kitchen when I should be working on my book … what is *wrong* with me?' We have become so programmed to produce and do and be *busy* and productive, it's no wonder self-loathing is attached to the process of procrastination.

I started reading up about procrastination and I realised that I could learn to use my procrastination habits as a clue to my state of mind, and to ultimately help manage my productivity in a healthier way. Because pouring buckets of scathing self-loathing over myself over and over again was, surprise surprise, not really working for me.

So what is procrastination? What are some of the reasons behind why we do it? Can we learn to wake ourselves up from procrastination paralysis and just *get started*? In our world of do, do, do and produce, produce, produce, there has to be room for a little breathing space, right? Is procrastination ever a good thing?

What I've found, as a seasoned procrastinator, is that often the most perfect thing to do is *start*. So, let's get going.

THE INSTANT GRATIFICATION MONKEY

Tim Urban is a writer and co-founder of the hilarious yet helpful procrastination website waitbutwhy.com. His description of the murky waters of procrastination is perhaps my favourite piece of writing on the subject.[10] Urban thinks of procrastination as an instant gratification monkey taking control of your brain, rendering the rational decision-maker, who steers your internal ship sensibly and with your best interests at heart, powerless. The instant gratification monkey loves YouTube spirals and spending hours clicking through each picture in the photo albums of one of your forgotten old flames on Facebook, but is also good at tricking the rational decision-maker into thinking that reorganising the To Do list for the twelfth time is actually productive.

Urban's piece, complete with stick-figure drawings, feels like a map of the inside of my brain when I'm in a procrastination doom loop, heading towards procrastination paralysis.

In his 2011 book *Thinking, Fast and Slow*, Nobel laureate and psychologist Daniel Kahneman lays out the theories that he has developed over decades' worth of research on cognitive biases and happiness, in collaboration with his friend and colleague Amos Tversky. A central theme is the exploration of two modes of thought, which Kahneman refers to as System 1 and System 2, and how they affect our decision-making.[11]

System 1 is a fast way of thinking. It's emotionally charged and subconscious. The instant gratification monkey thinks in System 1. He never graduates to the System 2 mode of thinking, which is slow, intentional, logical and conscious.

System 2 sounds like a good place to work from, doesn't it? I'm drawn to the idea of this slower, more intentional way of thinking because, to me, it represents the space I've been searching for in my own approach to work. We don't always need to use System 2. When we're brushing our teeth, for example, or going for a walk. It's subconscious.

But, as Kahneman sees it, it's too *hard* to be thoughtful at work or life, to mindfully move towards System 2, when System 1 might have a much quicker, easier response. When we're under pressure at work, it's only too easy to make decisions from that fast, reactive place rather than from a slower, more thoughtful place. This means that the instant gratification monkey can easily take control of the ship.

SO MANY FEELINGS

But why? Why do we let the monkey take control? Why do we procrastinate? It's easy to blame our poor time management skills or even berate ourselves for being lazy. But what if the monkey is just a front to distract you from a truckload of under-the-surface emotions? It could be argued that the monkey is trying to protect you from having to think too deeply about your feelings. Because feelings are hard and cute cat videos are easy. For me, those feelings can include fear of failure (or fear of success), perfectionism, expectations, control and overwhelm. Let's take a closer look, shall we?

Feeling 1: Fear of failure

Most of my project processes go like this:

1.   Woohoo! This is such an exciting project and I am just so thrilled with my life. I can *do* this.

21

2. Wow, OK, there's actually quite a lot to do ... and there's actually quite a lot of new stuff that I don't know which I'll have to learn ...

3. I can't do any of this. Why did I take this on? Why have I done this to myself *again*? Why don't I just *play it safe*?

4. I absolutely can *not* do this. *cries and throws self on sofa in front of episodes of *Ru Paul's Drag Race* and/or *Star Trek: The Next Generation**

5. Oh ... wait, I think I get it now. I think I know how to do this. Yes. OK. I got this.

6. *Upon project completion which (surprise!) was a success* This has been such an exciting project and I am so thrilled with having accomplished it. Woohoo! Now, where is my next challenge?

The fear of the empty page, or the thesis yet to be researched, or the project yet to be properly planned, can be utterly debilitating. For many of us, a fear of failure is a key element in our pull towards procrastination, and psychologists have shown us that it goes much deeper than just stalling projects at the outset, middle or end.

In their deeply insightful book, *Procrastination: Why You Do It, What To Do About It* (published in 1983 and revised in

2008), Dr Jane Burka and Dr Lenora Yuen talk about fear of failure among other procrastination motivators. The book looks at the psychology of procrastination as well as offering some helpful tips on avoiding the procrastination doom loop.

'People who have inhibited themselves because of their fear of failing tend to define "failure" in a very broad way,' write Burka and Yuen. 'When they are disappointed by their performance on a task, they think not only have they failed on that task, but also that they have failed as a person.'[12]

Blindboy Boatclub is an artist, comedian, and part of the satirical Irish comedy hip-hop duo The Rubberbandits. He's gas, but he's also wicked smart, with a special interest in mental health and emotional intelligence. He has a Master's in Psychology predating The Rubberbandits days and, over the course of a conversation I have with him about procrastination, he explains his view on why we procrastinate even when we are passionate about our work:

'The root of all procrastination,' says Blindboy, ' is the fear of failure. I mean, sometimes we procrastinate because it's a really boring piece of work so we just don't want to do it. But when you're procrastinating with your passion, it's because you're afraid of failure. The key to getting around that fear is to look at how you construct your identity and your self-esteem.

So, if it was important that people believe I was a very funny comedian or a great musician – if my identity is invested in that – then failing doesn't mean failing at a particular task, it means failing as a human being. So the risks are actually quite massive. Procrastination is how we protect ourselves from that pain.'

Carol Dweck, Professor of Psychology at Stanford University and author of the 2006 book *Mindset: The New Psychology of Success*, has a similar approach to understanding procrastination. Dweck identifies two key ways of thinking and being: fixed and growth mindsets. According to Dweck's research, people with fixed mindsets believe that their talents and attributes are fixed, which might leave them to wonder 'Is what I have enough?' Those with growth mindsets believe that their personal attributes can be developed through effort and learning, so that they can always improve with hard work.[13] Which mindset do you think harbours a fear of failure?

According to Dweck, for a person with a fixed mindset, making a mistake isn't just seen as an isolated incident. Instead, it's a reflection of their person as a whole. The 'I made a mistake' can easily spiral into 'I'm a complete failure. In every way.' These are really high stakes. No wonder we put off or avoid altogether work that brings up these feelings.

Reading through Dweck's book or indeed her website (www. mindsetonline.com) you might recognise parts of yourself in her fixed mindset template. I certainly did. And, according to Dweck, there are a host of reasons why people like me and perhaps people like you have developed that fixed mindset, such as being well-intentionally praised for talent over effort as children. The good news is, Dweck claims, that we can retrain our brains and embrace a growth mindset. We'll come back to Dweck's ideas later in this book and learn how to put some of this into practice.

For chronic procrastinators, delaying projects until the last minute helps to avoid having to face the truth of our talent and skills. 'Oh well, if I'd started it earlier or really put my best efforts in, then it would have been amazing but I left it to the last minute so ... that's why it's just a regular slightly above-average piece of work.' By continuously procrastinating, we never have to find out that our best work might just be a regular slightly above-average piece of work, particularly if we've built our identity around being smart or talented. Being faced with the idea that you might be just above average after all is too terrifying a prospect. Better not to try at all.

As Burka and Yuen put it, 'Procrastination allows people to take comfort in believing that their ability is greater than their performance indicates, perhaps even maintaining the belief that they are brilliant or unlimited in their potential to do well.' Oh, brother.

'The greatest things I've learned have been from failures,' says Blindboy. 'You can't learn anything from six months of doing nothing, but you can learn loads from six months of failure. The only failure you can't take value from is the failure of having not tried,' he says. 'That's the real kick in the balls.'

Feeling 2: Fear of success

Um … what? How could anyone be afraid of success? Author, educational psychologist and executive coach Russell Bishop has a wellbeing column in the *Huffington Post*. He writes: 'When confronting the myriad challenges we face in life, one oft-overlooked limiting factor might just be what some have called "the fear of success". Fear of success and fear of failure can be very closely aligned.'

Initially, it might sound odd to have a fear of success. Isn't success the very thing we're all constantly encouraged to seek out and create for ourselves? But sit back and have a think about it. In an office environment, you might be worried about succeeding too much in case your already over-demanding boss starts piling more work on you. Better to play it safe rather than show them how much you can really do, and risk having too many people relying on you.

Or you might be afraid that you won't be able to cope with the pressure of maintaining success. If you think about it, apart from the emotional trauma, being a 'failure' is kind of easy. You just stay in the same place, never achieving your goals, watching endless episodes of *Gilmore Girls* in your pyjamas ... Success, once achieved, has to be maintained. What if you succeed and then you're finally outed as an imposter? Ever-rising stakes and increasing pressure are the price of success. It's scary up there.

A fear of failure or success is a complex and deeply personal issue that could be guiding your decisions without your conscious awareness. It's possible that a therapist or a life coach might help you unpack some of your notions around success. Maybe you have a block around success that needs to be unplugged? Your procrastination habits could provide the clue that leads you towards a better sense of yourself and your motivations.

Feeling 3: Perfectionism

Think about the term 'perfectionism'. Do you think of this as a negative or a positive state? In a world of celebrity obsession, fad diets and aggressive marketing campaigns, the notion of perfection is still seen as a goal, as something to strive for and to aspire to. 'My greatest weakness is that I'm a perfectionist,' gulps the nervous job interviewee, fooling no one.

Perfectionism is commonly identified as manifesting itself in two forms: adaptive and maladaptive perfectionism. Adaptive perfectionism is seen as a healthy, motivated drive for high standards. Maladaptive perfectionism is the one you have to watch out for, as this is what your Inner Critic feeds off. This type of perfectionism constantly undermines you by having outrageously unrealistic goals and impossibly high standards for yourself, standards that you would never in a million years ask another person to hold themselves to.

It's possible that you are a perfectionist if you:

▷ Cannot cope with making mistakes, no matter how teeny tiny they might seem to others;

▷ Are unreasonably hard on yourself and hold yourself to standards that you wouldn't hold someone else to;

▷ Are deeply terrified of failure – so afraid that it makes the process of a project almost unbearable;

▷ Have low self-esteem;

▷ Are defensive about your own abilities and find criticism (even constructive criticism) devastating.

In a 2013 lecture on perfectionism for the School of Life in London, Carol Dweck said that 'people in a fixed mindset believe that effort is only for the imperfect. If you're really good at something, you shouldn't have to work hard on it. I think this is the worst belief that anyone could have. Everything important in life requires huge amounts of effort over long periods of time. If effort makes you feel inadequate, you're at a huge disadvantage.'[14]

Perfectionism is a classic fixed mindset trait, as there's a constant need to prove that you are without fault. That you are perfect. Because in the fixed mindset, as Dweck argues, you are what you are and one mistake or failure is a reflection on your entire being.

'Many procrastinators do not realise that they are perfectionists,' writes philosopher John Perry in his book *The Art of Procrastination: A Guide To Effective Dawdling, Lollygagging and Postponing*, 'for the simple reason that they have never done anything perfectly or even nearly so. They have never been told that something they did was perfect. They have never themselves felt that anything they did was perfect. They think, quite mistakenly, that being a perfectionist implies often, or sometimes, or at least once, having completed some task to perfection. But this is a misunderstanding of the basic dynamic of perfectionism. Perfectionism is a matter of fantasy, not reality.'[15]

So what if we aimed to be imperfectionists, instead of perfectionists? In *How to Be an Imperfectionist*, the writer and recovering perfectionist Stephen Guise outlines ways in which we can identify perfectionism in ourselves and stop it holding us back, such as when it fuels procrastination. Guise recommends an approach of caring less, but being very specific about what we choose to care less about.

For example, we should care less about the results, and care more about the process. He makes the distinction that 'perfectionists use their desire for positive results to motivate them to go through the process' whereas 'imperfectionists focus on the process and let the results take care of themselves.'[16] The idea of 'focus on the process, not the results' has become a personal mantra for me, and I've found it really does help. It helped me to write this book.

Goals are what drive us. We need them. It's not that it's unhealthy to aim big and have a daydream about being on *The Ellen Show* (I just *really* want to dance with her and tell her about Sing Along Social), but when our perfectionist tendencies inflate the power of our Inner Critic by focusing on an unrealistic result (e.g. writing the Best Book Ever or being the Best Project Manager Ever), that's when our process can become derailed and we become susceptible to tumbling down the rabbit hole of procrastination.

Now, when I find my mind starting to spin with worries about the end result, I take a deep breath and say to myself: 'Focus on the process, not the result.' It helps bring my attention back to the work in front of me, as opposed to an imaginary and unreal catastrophic future that might not ever happen.

A note on the perfect environment

'I need to make a cup of coffee before I do anything,' I'll say to myself at the beginning of my work day. 'You know what,' I'll think as I sit down to my desk with a freshly brewed cup of coffee in my hand, 'I should be wearing my *other* pair of glasses to write this.' I'll spend a few minutes looking for my other glasses, even though both glasses, apart from their frames, are identical. 'This room is a bit messy,' I'll think as I look around, taking a sip of coffee, wearing my other pair of glasses. 'I'll just give it a quick tidy up before I get started.'

The need to have the perfect environment in which to work is a classic procrastination trope. Sure, a lot of CEOs and productivity coaches note their routines, particularly their morning routines, as a secret to their productivity, such as Richard Branson's blog post 'Why I Wake Up Early'.[17] Whether it's starting the day with a cup of coffee or using a productivity method like the Pomodoro Technique or lighting a scented candle on your desk to signify that it's time to work, routines can be enormously helpful in focusing our minds into work mode. It's also true that some of us are more productive in the morning and others do their best work in the afternoon or evening.

These are all really useful pieces of information to know about ourselves, and to learn how to work with. However, becoming too rigid around these sets of circumstances can create the grounds for procrastination indulgence. 'Oh, look, it's already past 11am and I do my best writing work in the morning,' I'll say to myself, as if I don't know exactly what I'm doing. 'I guess I'll simply have to wait until tomorrow to write more of my book. Oh, well, time to check in with Jean-Luc Picard, I guess.'

So yes, get to know what kind of environment and set of circumstances help you to work at your best. But be aware of a reliance on creating the perfect environment in which to work and just make sure you're not using it as a way to justify a bout of unproductive procrastination. Don't underestimate how clever you are when it comes to finding ways to procrastinate. If you're anything like me, you're practically at genius levels when it comes to finding ways of getting out of doing something you don't want to do, or are afraid to do.

Feeling 4: Overwhelm

'I'm just ... so overwhelmed.' How many times have you said this to yourself or others in the last month?

Feeling overwhelmed can be a thoroughly effective productivity killer. At peak overwhelm, sometimes it feels that the only option is procrastination, particularly if it's the type of overwhelm that stems from a fear of failure rather than a more straightforward need to take on less work.

Over email, I confided in my friend Kristin Jensen, a food writer and cookbook editor, that I was feeling a bit overwhelmed at the prospect of putting together this book. She told me the title story from *Bird by Bird*, a book about creativity and life by the American writer Anne Lammot. The book's title comes from a memory from Lammot's childhood when her older brother was 10 years old. He had put off a school assignment, a report about birds, for an entire summer, leaving it until the night before the first day of school. 'He was at the kitchen table close to tears,' writes Lammot, 'surrounded by binder paper and pencils and unopened books on birds, immobilized by the hugeness of the task ahead. Then my father sat down beside him, put his arm around my brother's shoulder, and said, "Bird by bird, buddy. Just take it bird by bird."'[18]

The fear of failure, maladaptive perfectionism and unrealistic expectations are all great for making a person feel overwhelmed. They're massive themes. It's no wonder we go for the easy option of watching *The Gilmore Girls* to avoid having to face up to them.

But what if your feelings of overwhelm are actually stemming from the fact that you have too much on your plate? Have you simply taken on too much? Do you *whispers* *need help*? Over-achievers and people who love to work are absolute divils when it comes to taking on too much or taking on projects that come at too high a price to their wellbeing.

Is it possible that you're procrastinating because you are concerned that you can't do the job? Not because you are afraid of failure but because it is literally impossible to do what you have on your plate and no person on earth (apart from Michelle Obama, of course) could manage it?

You might not be procrastinating at all. You might simply be *wrecked*. Out of fuel. Battery dead. When you are knee-deep in deadlines, tasks and firefighting emails, it can feel impossible to take a break. That is a lie. And it's a lie you need to un-tell yourself, with great urgency. It's time to realise that taking breaks is *part of your job*. It will make you *better* at your job. We'll be talking a little more about the importance of recovery time later in this book, so keep in mind the role that procrastination might play in forcing you to take breaks.

CAN PROCRASTINATION BE A GOOD THING?

We tend to think of procrastination in negative terms perhaps because of how rotten it feels to be trapped in a procrastination doom loop of dread and fear of failure. It stings! But, apart from when it might be a sign of overwhelm, is it possible that procrastination might have other useful messages for us?

We all have to do things we don't want to do. I hate carrying things, but sometimes I can't avoid carrying shopping bags back from a grocery shop. I hate doing my taxes but I simply have to get them done. Neither task is ever as bad as I had predicted. Well, maybe carrying the shopping bags. Carrying heavy things sucks.

But what about when we don't want to do something at work? Do we have a choice in the matter?

Sometimes, procrastination can be a way of signalling that this is not what we want to be doing with our lives. 'Of course!' I can hear you say. But our minds are crafty and sometimes it's not that obvious that you don't want to do something. For example, I have taken on pieces of work that I knew I wasn't interested in. I just felt like I couldn't say no to the person asking so I agreed to take them on, spent an agonising three months procrastinating, before finally doing a grand job in the end. The point is, I didn't want to do it but I didn't know that at the outset. I wasn't ready to listen to my gut.

Anne Marie Downey is a pharmacist, DJ and addiction counsellor. I interviewed her for an *Irish Times* article on the subject of procrastination. 'The reasons you procrastinate are as unique as you are,' she told me.

'Getting to know yourself and your own patterns is what it's about. Are you setting unrealistic expectations on yourself? If you find the thought of making changes overwhelming, they probably are. When I notice procrastination in myself I don't criticise, I prioritise. I recognise I have limited time and resources so I ask myself, "What right now is most important to me?" I take it as an opportunity to turn my awareness towards it, whatever it is, and to see what's really going on. If I find myself getting really stuck, I reach out. Life is here to be lived, flawed reality and all.'

If you're puzzled as to why you haven't started a project or a piece of work, and feel a baffling reluctance to do it, maybe you need to ask yourself a few questions about it. Do you actually care about this task? Is it important? Is it necessary? Do you *want* to do it? Can you make a choice to *not* do this? If you're not interested, what does it tell you about your current situation? Is it a sign that you should move on or stop doing this type of work?

Granted, having a choice in whether you do a piece of work or not is more likely if you are a freelancer. But maybe there's a way you can talk to your manager or boss if you are consistently procrastinating on particular tasks. Can you get some support in this area?

Procrastination vs percolation

Have you ever watched coffee percolate, where the coffee drips gradually through a filter into a pot? If you want a *good* cup of coffee, as opposed to instant (yuk!), then you might have to invest a few minutes of your time. It's not a case of flicking a switch and, boom, you've got a cup of coffee. There's a process involved.

If we think of our outputs at work as a carefully brewed cup of coffee and our creative process as the coffee pot, the idea of procrastination takes on a new aroma. Knowing the difference between procrastination (when you're putting an action off because of a fear of failure or overwhelm) and percolation (when your idea is still bubbling away in the coffee pot and just isn't ready to be served yet) can save the percolating worker a world of angst.

The singer-songwriter Lisa O'Neill has fine-tuned her relationship with procrastination and percolation. She told me a story about a particularly unsuccessful day she'd had. She had set out to write a new song but it didn't come together. She gave up and instead spent the day cooking a stew for her flatmate. She went out to a nearby market to get ingredients, walking along the Grand Canal and thinking about the song she was working on, worrying a bit that she wasn't actively working on it.

By the time she and her flatmate sat down to the stew, she confided that she was feeling she had kind of wasted her day. 'But this stew is delicious,' said her flatmate. 'This is a creative stew!' Lisa realised that she had needed that day of nourishment, a day to nourish herself and someone else. The song came together the next day.

Steve McCarthy is a Dublin-based designer, illustrator and bearded gentleman. He has worked as a key background designer for the Oscar-nominated feature film *Song of the Sea* and has brought the words of award-winning children's books to life through illustration. Procrastination is one of his favourite subjects to ponder:

'I feel like I have a finite amount of creative energy to work with every day, and starting something takes a lot of juice. Procrastinating to me is about getting a run at something. It's about timing. When you start to think of procrastination as a volatile force, like anger, you can learn to funnel it into positive places. I also recognise that I have chosen a profession that is built around the percolation of ideas. It's what I do all day, so there's no reason not to look forward to it, so I have allowed myself to geek out about the details. I try and make the process of procrastination an integral part of my day. I do this by making it tactile, because I enjoy that: timers, post its, lists, white boards etc. I'm aware it's an indulgence and I try to lean into it.'

It can be really confusing when you find yourself procrastinating in a job that you love. I think these stories speak to the idea that work doesn't have to be go, go, go and produce, produce, produce. A lot of jobs outside the traditional creative arts of music, comedy and design involve creative thinking, such as architecture, advertising, software development and teaching. Any small business owner, whether they're a farmer or run a taxi company, has to use creative thinking to make their business stand out from the crowd. Allowing ourselves the space to replenish ideas or room to nourish inspiration isn't just for painters, songwriters and comedians.

Companies around the world have implemented formal programmes to allow their employees time to breathe, with varying degrees of success. Perhaps the most famous is Google's 20% time, launched by founders Larry Page and Sergey Brin in 2004, with the idea that employees had permission to 'spend 20% of their time working on what they think will most benefit Google ...' in addition to their regular projects.

At an all-employee meeting at Yahoo, the company's CEO and former Googler Marissa Meyer is reported to have said that she wasn't going to implement a 20% time at Yahoo. Her reason? 'I've got to tell you the dirty little secret of Google's 20% time. It's really 120% time.'[19] So, a great idea that didn't quite work in implementation. Google officially scrapped this policy in 2013, but other companies maintain their efforts to provide space at work for creative downtime, such as internal work programmes like LinkedIn's InCubator and Apple's Blue Sky. After five years of working at Thinkhouse, one of Ireland's most successful youth marketing agencies, employees are given a month off to 're-energise, explore the world and come back with a bang.'

Our working world is geared up to focusing on the result, but sometimes the process calls for a little bit of percolation. Emma Norton is Head of Development for Element Pictures, the Irish production company behind films such as *The Lobster* and the Oscar-winning *Room*. 'Film development is notoriously slow work,' Norton tells me. People can work on films for years before they get made and though there may be short deadlines within that time, such as for funding, development can be a long game.

'Like a lot of jobs, the challenge of developing something well is in focusing properly and not just trying to get to the next step and tick off the task. So sometimes when the list of jobs that day is getting longer and the emails keep interrupting your flow, it's tempting to rush off the script notes and then get them sent out. But the key to good development is thinking time, so there is also a lot of discussion and then writing itself slows things down and then there are bus journeys to sit and think about all the little niggles that eventually work their way into your notes. So the challenge is to resist the desire to rush.'

You might be thinking to yourself that you don't have the luxury of procrastinating because of your job circumstances or your boss or the pressure you are under. But regardless of your circumstances, I hope you can relate to the notion of letting your ideas have a bit of breathing space, and not getting so worked up when the ideas don't pop out of you fully formed. Knowing the difference between when you are procrastinating and when your ideas are merely percolating is a life skill, and an important one to hone.

Procrastiwork

What do you do when you're procrastinating? When I'm deep in the doom loop, I'm good for nothing but Netflix and cracker consumption. But there is another type of procrastination that is a much happier, healthier and even productive place that's known in some circles as 'procrastiwork'.

The American lettering artist and author Jessica Hische coined this glorious phrase. In her definition of procrastiwork, she explained that 'the work you do when you procrastinate is probably the work you should be doing for the rest of your life'.

Before I worked as a creative events planner, a procrastination tactic I employed was to *plan*. Planning elaborate treasure hunts around Dublin city for a special friend's birthday. Implementing a pop-up restaurant hen party for my beloved sister. Developing multi-course menus for a dinner party with pals. These were all things I did when I probably should have been working on something else.

I was 110% procrastinating on a writing deadline when I came up for the idea of what would become the Sing Along Social.

This zero-commitment choir turned out to be one of the most rewarding and fun projects I've ever created. I indulged in the idea of getting a group of people together to sing along to Alanis Morisette's *Jagged Little Pill* from start to finish when I *really* should have been working on an article. I still got the article submitted in time for print, but in the meantime I had laid the groundwork for what has become a source of income and, more important, a fountain of great happiness for me and perhaps even for the caterwaulers in my chaotic choir of craic.

What do *you* do when you're procrastinating? Is there any way you can make that more of a full-time gig? Are you obsessed with organising your cupboards? Maybe you should look into becoming a professional organiser. Pay attention to what you do when you're procrastinating in case it gives you a window into what you should *really* be doing with your life.

From the outside looking in, I may not seem like a procrastinator. I do a lot of stuff. All the time. But the truth is that procrastination is one of the secrets to my productivity. I'm often doing something because I'm trying to avoid doing something else, making me a very productive procrastinator.

In order to delay The Big Thing, the productive procrastinator does a million other things. This skillful procrastinator can be so adept at avoiding The Big Thing by putting their energy into other tasks, they might even garner a reputation as someone who Gets Things Done.

The philosopher John Perry calls this 'structured procrastination'. In *The Art of Procrastination*, he outlines what he sees as a way of harnessing the perceived flaw of procrastination. 'To make structured procrastination work for you, begin by establishing a hierarchy of the tasks you have to do, in order of importance from the most urgent to the least important. Even though the most important tasks are on top, you have worthwhile tasks to perform lower on the list. Doing those tasks becomes a way of not doing the things higher on the list. With this sort of appropriate task structure, you can become a useful citizen. Indeed, the procrastinator can even acquire, as I have, a reputation for getting a lot done.'

The Art of Procrastination actually started life as a shorter essay Perry wrote when he was supposed to be correcting his students' papers and reviewing draft dissertations. In the essay, he shared a story of how he used to procrastinate on grading papers and preparing lectures when he was a resident fellow in one of the Stanford University dorms. Instead of doing his work, he would head over and hang out with the students.

'I got a reputation for being a *terrific* resident fellow, one of the rare profs on campus who spent time with undergraduates and got to know them. What a setup: Play Ping-Pong as a way of not doing more important things, and get a reputation as Mr Chips.'

Pretty productive, right?

EAT THE FROG

As I've been learning more about my own personal relationship with procrastination, I've been mindful to not be too indulgent about it. It's our responsibility to manage our time and to make sure we get our work done on time. But knowing when and when not to indulge in the sweet, tortuous guilty pleasure of procrastination is a seriously useful life skill. Equally, knowing when we need a break or that our ideas just need more time to percolate is very grown-up too.

Have you ever heard the motivation expression 'eat the frog'? It comes from something Mark Twain is reported to have said: 'Eat a live frog first thing in the morning and nothing worse will happen to you the rest of the day.'

In terms of work motivation, the frog is another word for the Big Thing. The Scary Project. The Dread-Drenched Deadline.

Eating the frog is the method of just tackling that horrible, scary project first thing in the morning, before you even look at your emails. Get it done before you've had the chance to procrastinate and the worst is out of the way.

Have you ever put something off and then put it off a little more until the dread of The Thing looms heavy over all aspects of your life? And then have you ever found that once you get going on The Thing that The Thing actually wasn't all that bad to begin with and actually you *can* do it and you're even enjoying it? This brings me to another personal mantra: 'action cures fear'. Much like overcoming Sunday Night Fear, if you can talk yourself down from the ledge and get started, you might just find that The Thing is not such a big Thing after all.

After all, the most perfect thing to do is *start*.

FIVE SLOW NOTES TO SELF ....

Here are a few strategies I have learned to use to help me navigate my penchant for procrastination in a slower, more compassionate way.

1. Focus on the process, not the result.

Tucked away in a drawer in my desk is a little notebook which I can easily access in case of emergencies. On one of the pages I have written a couple of phrases that are helpful little mantras that I can use to reassure myself and quell the rising overwhelm before it consumes me. These little phrases have all successfully helped me navigate the procrastination doom loop, with a pretty high success rate. Included in the scribbles in this notebook are:

▷ Focus on the process, not the result;
▷ Bird by bird;
▷ 'Good Enough' is good enough because perfect doesn't exist;
▷ The most perfect thing to do is start;
▷ Action cures fear.

2. Be nice to yourself.

When I'm feeling overwhelmed, the things I find most helpful are:

▷ Getting away from my desk and going for a walk;
▷ Throwing a ball for my dog and marvelling at just how completely in the moment she is;
▷ Talking to my husband, my sister or a friend about it.

3. Get to know your Inner Critic.

If you, like me, struggle with a fear of failure and maladaptive perfectionism, it's possible your Inner Critic is a skilled collaborator in your unhealthy procrastination patterns.

▷ Get to know your Inner Critic and its patterns. When I discovered my Inner Critic didn't seem to be active early in the mornings, I started getting up early to write. That way I got a headstart and outsmarted my debilitating Inner Critic.

4. Feed your mind.

▷ Be honest with yourself. You know deep down the difference between procrastination and percolation. Know when to feed your mind and take a break and know when to just get on with it.

▷ Conversations, books, films and articles can all feed into your work, even if it's *gasp* stuff you enjoy.

▷ Is your idea ready to reveal itself? Maybe you need some percolation time.

5. Just eat the fecking frog.

▷ Turn off all your social media notifications so you can avoid distractions.

▷ Limit your email time and use an out-of-office notice if you have to.

▷ Switch off your internet completely. Just. Turn. It. Off.

▷ Do some research around productivity apps or software that might help. For example: an app I find really helpful is the Pomodoro Technique, which is based on 25-minute bursts of work. It gets its name from the tomato kitchen timer.

▷ Start your work without ceremony. This is when you can just start anytime, anywhere as opposed to needing your cup of coffee, your correct pair of glasses, the right chair at the right desk on the right day in order to get any work done. Your work environment is unlikely to ever be exactly perfect, so don't rely too heavily on work touchstones.

SLOW READS ....

Here are my favourite books on the subject of procrastination, which have really helped enable me to put off writing this chapter.

• *Mindset* by Carol Dweck

• *Procrastination: Why You Do It, and What To Do About It* by Dr Jane B Burka and Dr Lenora M Yuen

• *The Art of Procrastination: A Guide to Effective Dawdling, Lollygagging and Postponing* by John Perry

TWO

Imposter

'Y ou can't write a book about work. You're not an organisational psychologist. You're barely even a writer. And what do you know about the struggles facing people who work anyway? Most days, your work involves travelling around the country giving out about speciality coffee and ruminating on mediocre toasted cheese sandwiches. Why are you even *pretending* to try to string words together when you know you have nothing to say and no authority with which to say it? Somebody else would write this book way better than you could.'

A bully I know *actually* said all of this (and many variations of it) to me. In person. Before and during the process of writing this book. It might be hard to believe that a moderately successful, relatively intelligent woman with a great support network of family and friends like myself would put up with this kind of shit from a bully. But I do, and have done for years, almost on a daily basis. You know why? Because the bully is me.

My Inner Critic is such a large part of my life and I know her so intimately that I'm on first name terms with her. I call her Aunt Linda. She's a real piece of work.

Aunt Linda, like most Inner Critics, is *really* good at selling Imposter Syndrome, and making it seem very real. She's the voice behind the feeling that you're a fraud. She's the voice that tells you that you are useless. That you're going to fail. That nobody likes you. Aunt Linda says unspeakable things to you that you wouldn't *dream* of saying to anyone else. If you suffer from a particularly cruel Inner Critic, like my Aunt Linda, you'll know how debilitating it can be.

But here's the thing. Just as you can choose how you react to and interact with an unpleasant person in your circle of friends or family who has a knack for making you feel crap about yourself, I can choose how I react to my fictional Aunt Linda. This chapter is about Imposter Syndrome and its great friend the Inner Critic. We're going to look at whether it's possible to have a slower, more compassionate approach to absorbing internal and external criticism. How can we differentiate between the Inner Critic's voice and the truth? Can we learn to live with our Aunt Lindas?

THE INNER CRITIC

Let me tell you about Aunt Linda. She is a lemon-faced meanie with severe resting bitch face who has nothing good to say about anything or anyone.

Aunt Linda is an entirely fictional character I created, loosely based on Kristen Wiig's *Saturday Night Live* character of the same name, a cranky woman in her 50s who gives grumpy movie reviews. I should clarify that my real-life aunts are all lovely. Creating Aunt Linda came about on the advice of my therapist, who helped me to see that even though Aunt Linda is a total wagon, she is also a member of my family and deep down has my best interests at heart. Aunt Linda is trying to save me from making a fool of myself. She would prefer I did *nothing* rather than trying and failing publicly.

What the Aunt Linda character helped me do is externalise the criticisms, and it took a bit of the sting out of the Inner Critic's words. It also helped me to realise how often Aunt Linda was talking to me; her voice was like a running commentary in my head, telling me how terrible I was. Creating this character made my fears feel less overwhelming, less *true*, and reminded me that the Inner Critic is just one voice and isn't the whole truth about my experience.

As I got to know Aunt Linda a little better, I started to notice that she had patterns. She would show up in certain situations, such as when I was working with people I really respected and who I felt had more qualifications/talent/drive than I did. After some observation, I noticed that she didn't seem to wake up before noon. If I started work early, before 8 am, I could get almost a full day of work done before she had even stirred.

The Aunt Linda method doesn't have a 100% success rate. Sometimes the Inner Critic wins and I can be paralysed by fear. But paying attention to when she showed up meant I was better able to understand the issues that I needed to work on. For me, those included a deeply rooted fear of failure – thanks, in part, to a strong streak of perfectionism. Is it possible that, underneath its cruel demeanour, your Inner Critic is trying to protect you from something? And is that something a real or imagined threat?

The Inner Critic has plenty of different names. Some psychologists call it the critical inner voice. The comedian Amy Poehler calls it her demon. The author Seth Godin calls it the Lizard Brain, in reference to its connection to the ancient function in our brains known as fight or flight, powered by the amygdala in the limbic system. 'The Inner Critic, on an inner level, is the source of low self-esteem,' Hal and Sirda Stone wrote in their book *Embracing Your Inner Critic: Turning Self-Criticism Into A Creative Asset.*[20]

Speaking to Sarah Green Carmichael as part of the *Harvard Business Review*'s IdeaCast podcast, Tara Mohr talks about the themes she delves into in her book *Playing Big: Practical Wisdom for Women Who Want to Speak Up, Create and Lead*. In the short interview, Mohr sums up the quality of the Inner Critic very clearly.

'Your Inner Critic is very different from your voice of critical thinking or realistic thinking … The way that we can tell apart the Inner Critic voice in us from the voice of realistic thinking or positive critical thinking really has to do with the tone of the thoughts in our head. So the Inner Critic will tend to be very repetitive and like a broken record, saying the same thing over again. It might be "there's no way this is going to work. There's no way this is going to work. There's no way this is going to work", let's say, if you're starting a new venture. If it's talking to you in a way that is harsher and meaner than you would want to speak to someone you love, you're hearing the Inner Critic.'[21]

There are theories that we humans are in fact hard-wired to respond to the negative, and that we are programmed to hear negatives louder than positives. Psychologist and author of *Hardwiring Happiness*, Dr Rick Hanson, writes about 'Confronting the Negativity Bias' on his website.

'The alarm bell of your brain – the amygdala – uses about two-thirds of its neurons to look for bad news: it's primed to go negative. Once it sounds the alarm, negative events and experiences get quickly stored in memory – in contrast to positive events and experiences, which usually need to be held in awareness for a dozen or more seconds to transfer from short-term memory buffers to long-term storage.'[22]

So perhaps we have a primal need to seek out our Aunt Linda, but the trick is to learn how to identify her and how to work with her.

A CHAMPION? WHAT ARE YOU LOIKE?

My sister, Niamh, works for Google and lives in San Francisco. She is currently training to be a life coach. Her friend and colleague, Irene Patel, was also certifying as a coach and had agreed to give me a sample session over Skype. When she asked about my Inner Critic, I began to tell her with relish all about Aunt Linda. She interrupted before I had delivered the entire biopic. 'It sounds like you know your Inner Critic intimately,' she said. 'So, what does your champion look like?'

I paused. 'Um … my … champion? I guess it's … me?' I answered, unsure. I physically squinted my eyes trying to imagine the opposite of Aunt Linda but all I could see was a swirl of vague nothingness, with Aunt Linda standing right behind it, arms folded, with a stonkingly sour look on her face.

I realised that I had spent so much of my time with Aunt Linda that it had never occurred to me to create a character that could battle it out with her in my brain. A character that could perhaps fight for my attention and defend me against Aunt Linda's bullying.

The idea of creating a champion for myself feels like the most un-Irish thing ever. We are so adept at batting away compliments. 'You look really nice today, is that a new top?' 'This top? Oh my God, it's *disgusting*, I got it in Penneys, €5, I look awful.' (My mum, sister and I call this CPD: Compulsive Penneys Disclosure.) We have a tendency to play down our achievements for fear of being accused of having 'notions'. Because of this cultural trait, having an internal champion seems like the most ridiculous idea ever. I still haven't quite managed to properly commit to creating my champion character but I'm working on it.

In Ireland we often confuse confidence with having 'notions'. Having notions means you're a bit uppity, and it's basically one of the most offensive insults you could give an Irish person. The following are examples of what could be construed as signs of having notions:

▷ Having fancy statues on your suburban lawn.
▷ Drinking speciality coffee roasted nearby, brewed by a barista you know personally.
▷ Having a moustache any time after 1996.
▷ Calling yourself 'creative'.
▷ Eating artisanally produced cheese and delighting in locally cured chorizo.
▷ Saying 'I'm really good at that,' even if you actually really are good at that.

Contrary to what Irish culture might tell us, self-esteem is not a bad thing. My reluctance to create an Inner Champion character is connected to my blind fear of the possibility that I might start to have (God save us and bless us) notions about myself.

Is our fear of notions working for us any more? Or is it holding us back?

A thought is just a thought

At a creative conference called Swell Sligo, held in a former airport in the coastal town of Strandhill, I sat in what was once a departure lounge but was at that moment the venue for a lesson in present moment awareness with the life coach John Graham. Since that first session, I've learned a lot from John about negative thinking and ideas of perfectionism.

John is a Scotsman who moved to Ireland to work in the Learning & Development team of a large corporation, before following his gut and moving to Sligo, where he set up his own coaching practice (www.johngcoaching.com). He's really good at making mindfulness and meditation a forgiving process, and explaining it in a way that is really easy to grasp, particularly for beginners.

'A thought is just a thought,' he tells me, when I call him for a chat about the Inner Critic. It's good timing, because I'm feeling the fear of Imposter Syndrome when I speak to him. 'The Inner Critic is just a story we tell ourselves. It's a belief. But it's just a thought in the moment. When we pay attention to it and think that this voice is real, and that it has control over us, that's when we get in trouble with the Inner Critic.'

John has had his own experience with Imposter Syndrome. 'My life isn't perfect,' he tells me.

'I could ask myself, "Who am I to be dishing out advice to other people?" It was when I started to direct my attention to the results I was getting, rather than directing my attention to the *thoughts* I was having about the results I was getting, that I was able to get over that fear. It always comes back to the fact that a thought is just a thought.'

Remembering that your Inner Critic isn't real, that what it's saying isn't necessarily true, is an important step towards getting that cruel voice out of your head. How can we separate and disassociate ourselves from this inner voice, which can be deafening?

IMPOSTER PHENOMENON

In the late 1970s, clinical psychologist Dr Pauline Clance was teaching at a liberal arts college in the USA. She was surprised to hear echoes of the same fears she herself had had as an undergraduate from the students coming into her office for counselling. According to her website (www.paulineroseclance. com), one of her students said 'I feel like an imposter here with all these really bright people.' It was an 'Aha!' moment for Clance and, alongside her colleague Dr Suzanne Imes, she coined the term 'Imposter Phenomenon'. Together they wrote a seminal paper, published in 1978, entitled 'The imposter phenomenon in high achieving women: Dynamics and therapeutic intervention'.

Clance and Imes sampled primarily white middle- to upper-class women between the ages of 20 and 45, ranging in experience and positions from undergraduates to PhD faculty members to professional women. They found common themes in the childhood stories of the women they spoke to. Many of the women came from a family where another sibling was considered to be bright one or the star, so when they performed well as adults it felt like a case of mistaken identity. They were so used to the other sibling getting the praise.[23]

Women who had different upbringings could also grow up to feel like imposters. Their identity as the bright one or the star became a burden, something they felt they constantly had to live up to. It's easy for people with this kind of identity to feel phony. You're told your whole life that you're talented and exceptional and gifted. Then one day you realise that you actually have to work and study to maintain the ideal of being bright, special and talented. 'But I thought smart people didn't have to try ... I'm a fraud!'

Carol Dweck's book *Mindset* talks about the impact of praise on children and the incorrect idea that 'geniuses don't have to try'. Dweck's theory is that adults with a fixed mindset were most likely praised for their talents as children, receiving well-intentioned labels like 'genius' and 'gifted'. Adults with a growth mindset, on the other hand, were possibly praised more for their effort and hard work, reinforcing the idea that intelligence can be developed and is not a fixed state that one is born with. Imposter Syndrome thrives in a fixed mindset because this way of thinking makes space for the feeling of fraudulence.

Clance and Imes' study focused on women and noted that, though it appeared that men suffered less frequently from Imposter Syndrome, additional research needed to be done on the topic. In her book *Presence*, Harvard Business School professor and social psychologist Amy Cuddy recounts her experience of men and imposterism. 'Men experience imposterism to the same extent women do, they may be even more burdened by it because they can't admit it.' Cuddy feels that, because of a fear of experiencing 'stereotype backlash' when they don't act the way society wants them to (in this case, strong and fearless like the archetypal man), men carry their Imposter Syndromes around 'quietly, secretly, painfully', rather than telling anyone about it.[24]

Since Clance and Imes' research, a number of studies have found that Imposter Syndrome affects men and women from a variety of racial, cultural and professional backgrounds.

Actors, comedians, writers, CEOs, students, professors, medical students, neurosurgeons, musicians, astrophysicists … The experience of feeling like a fraud appears to be something almost everyone goes through at some point. And it's not just over-achievers who experience this. When Clance revisited the subject in a 1985 study with collaborator Gail Matthews, they found that 70% of the 41 men and women they looked at had felt like frauds at some point in their career.[25]

Are you doing this to yourself? Do you wonder when you're going to be found out, finally exposed as a complete fraud? Do you have a hard time accepting that you've done something well, or that you'll be able to repeat it? 'Fluke!' shouts your Inner Critic, delighting in bursting your tiny blossoming bubble of pride when you try to absorb an achievement.

When she spoke at the 2015 Harvard graduation ceremony, actress Natalie Portman said, 'When I came to Harvard Yard as a freshman in 1999, I felt like there had been some mistake … that every time I opened my mouth I would have to prove I wasn't just a dumb actress.'[26] She talked about how she viewed being an actor as not a serious enough occupation. She came from a family of academics, and acting seemed frivolous in comparison to academic pursuits.

As a student at Harvard she soon found herself plagued by self-doubt and overwhelmed by the challenges of academic life. After four years, she learned that acting was meaningful. It was *her* purpose. 'You can never be the best technically,' was one piece of advice she imparted in her speech. 'The only thing you can be the best at is developing your own self.'

In an odd sort of way, finding out that people you admire have the potential to feel as useless as you do is one of the few ways that comparing yourself to other people can actually be helpful. Imposter Syndrome is a big fat liar. *It's* the fraud, not us.

I'll never be as amazing as Michelle Obama

As the old saying goes, comparison is the thief of joy. If you're a perfectionist about your own expectations of yourself, it's possible that you might have an unrealistic idea of your role models. Instead of inspiring us, our ideas of how our role models achieved their goals can cause us to create impossible standards for ourselves.

We all have our role models (three of my favourites are Michelle Obama, Dolly Parton and Angela Lansbury) and often they inspire us to be better versions of ourselves. However, there are times when our role models can make us feel kind of crap about ourselves, particularly when we're already feeling a little crummy. For the perfectionist with a fixed mindset, the achievements of others are just another stick to beat ourselves with. If your confidence has taken a knock, looking at the success of others can be hard.

Looking at the perceived success of your peers, friends and family members can even make you feel jealous as well, which can be a bit of a shame spiral if you see yourself as someone who is supportive, kind and caring towards others. Being jealous doesn't fit in with that identity, does it?

It's quite possible you'll never be as amazing as Michelle Obama – because, I mean, she's *flawless* – but also because of the difference between your experience and hers. Obama had nearly 20 people working for her when she was First Lady of the United States.[27] In the 2010 White House Report to Congress, 18 people were identified as being part of Michelle's team, including a director of scheduling and events, a director of correspondence and a director of policy and projects.[28]

Do you have a director of correspondence? Does your director of scheduling and events have their own assistant? I didn't think so.

Comparing yourself to others and using your role models to highlight what isn't great about you, rather than looking to them as helpful ideals, is pure fodder for your devious Inner Critic.

You can't put a filter on a crisp sandwich

A good case study for not comparing ourselves to others is to look at how we use social media. I like to think that most of us have learned to take social media output with a pinch of salt. We have figured out that behind the beautifully curated scenes of perfection there is either a) a screaming baby in the background somewhere, b) a partner or pal who is getting really fed up at having to wait until after the photo has been taken for Insta to eat their dinner, only to find that it's gone cold, again, c) the unfeatured part of the kitchen/ bedroom/living area is a total shambles or d) all of the above.

The way I figured this out was because I looked at my own social media feed and saw how, whether consciously or unconsciously, I had edited out all the bad bits of my life. I've never posted on Twitter, Facebook or Instagram about worrying about money or feeling threatened by other people's success or that I couldn't get out of bed that day. I have posted exactly one photo of a crisp sandwich in the last three years, when in reality they play a much bigger role in my life. Think about how much you curate your own feed. The people on your feed that you're holding yourself up against may not be sharing all their bumps, bruises, warts and all.

The musician Sallay Matu Garnett, otherwise known as Loah, has had the experience of being an artist developing in the public eye by virtue of being a new artist in the digital age. Pre-internet, artists had more privacy to develop in the early stage of their career. Musicians today are quite visible and vulnerable.

'There's a weird duality between how we think we are perceived and how we are actually perceived,' says Matu Garnett. 'You're at home freaking out that you're never going to write another song again, and then you go out into the real world and people you meet are like "Hey, you're doing so well!" We put so much of the pressure on ourselves to create and put stuff out there. That pressure is self-generated and unnecessary. We're all doing it to each other. It's great that we celebrate each other's highlights but maybe we don't talk about each other's low times enough.'

Instead of focusing on the pressure that comes with being thought of as someone who is destined for greatness, Matu Garnett has stood her ground and focused on developing a strong sense of who she is as an artist, as well as not rushing the release of her first EP. This groundwork will no doubt pay off in her future career.

That duality of being perceived one way and thinking of yourself in another way is not unique to musicians under the pressure of 'making it'. Perhaps we can follow Matu Garnett's lead by going at our own pace and focusing on what our gut tells us is right for us? And not being afraid to admit when things *aren't* going so well.

THE EXTERNAL CRITIC

Dealing with a harsh Inner Critic is one thing, but how can we cope with criticism in the real world? For those of us who struggle with criticism and self-doubt, our relationships with internal and external criticism appear to have a lot in common, just like our old pals fear of failure and perfectionism. Can learning how to cope with the Inner Critic (which, for some of us, is the loudest critic we'll ever come across) help you face criticism or the fear of criticism in the world? I think so.

What is so terrifying about criticism (even the water-cooler gossip kind) or, for that matter, making mistakes and being wrong? Aren't we supposed to learn from constructive criticism? Don't we grow from our mistakes? For some of us, it's not quite that simple.

Dweck's theory of the fixed versus the growth mindset argues that those with a fixed mindset see criticism as an attack on their very identity and their core being. The criticism isn't just about the work, it's about the person: 'I did a bad job and therefore I am a bad person.' Whereas someone with a growth mindset can see mistakes as an opportunity to grow and learn, the person with a fixed mindset has an identity so perilously linked to their success that criticism is a real threat. If we are obsessed with getting praise from everyone about everything, we are going to fail. As long as you're not doing anything ethically questionable or something that could actively harm someone, whether someone thinks you are great or not shouldn't really concern you.

If we can free ourselves of the need to seek out praise, it is possible that we could quieten our Inner Critic and absorb external criticism in a healthy way.

INVITE AUNT LINDA TO THE PARTY, BUT BRUSH OFF HER BAD VIBES

In her memoir *Yes Please*, comedian Amy Poehler talks about her 'demon', the Inner Critic that tells her she is an untalented slob, and how she copes with that voice.

'When the demon starts to slither my way and say bad shit about me I turn around and say, "Hey. Cool it. Amy is my friend. Don't talk about her like that." Sticking up for ourselves in the same way we would one of our friends is a hard but satisfying thing to do. Sometimes it works.'[29]

The idea that you should only speak to yourself as you would to others is important. Why would you hold yourself up to different standards than you would someone else?

The author Tara Mohr talks about 'active noticing'. This is the first step towards realising when your Inner Critic is talking, as a way of separating it out from your more rational thoughts, which are usually a more accurate reflection of reality. She recommends you figure out what the Inner Critic might be trying to protect you from, and then accept that those negative thoughts are there – but that they might not necessarily be of any real use. For example, when your Inner Critic is telling you that you should give up and why bother and *don't do it*, is that your Inner Critic's way of trying to protect you from public failure?

Apart from distinguishing the Inner Critic from your more rational thoughts, discovering the possibility that the Inner Critic might be trying to help us is a powerful way of deactivating it. If I think about Aunt Linda as a member of my family, then I can open myself up to the idea that my mean old Aunt Linda actually loves me. Even if she has a really weird and hurtful way of showing it. But, as with real life family members, you are not obliged to take her advice and you can develop the skills of accepting who she is so that you can be around her without feeling triggered.

GOOD ENOUGH

As I outlined in the Procrastination chapter, I don't see perfectionism as an ideal to aspire to. On the contrary, it's turf for the fire that is inner criticism. If I'm a perfectionist who can't stand to make mistakes, how will I be able to achieve anything?

Maybe it's time to start embracing being Good Enough. American psychologist Barry Schwartz talks about the pressure that comes from a society based on an over-abundance of choice in his book *The Paradox of Choice: Why More Is Less*, and in a Ted Talk of the same name.[30]

He talks about 'choice overload', which makes us strive for perfection (we think, if there's so much choice, surely at least one of these is the perfect choice?) and makes us doubt our own decisions. It makes us unwilling to settle for less than perfect, which often leads to dissatisfaction and unhappiness. If we settle for Good Enough, especially in our world of too much, we're saving ourselves from the torment of making the best decision.

Is there space in your working life for Good Enough? It's hard for a perfectionist to let go of aspiring for perfection, but all the evidence seems to point to the fact that perfection is a myth.

ASTROPHYSICISTS FEEL LIKE IMPOSTERS, TOO

There is an important lesson to be learned from the story of Professor Dame Jocelyn Bell Burnell, the astrophysicist from Lurgan, Co Down. In her acceptance speech for an honorary degree from the Faculty of Science of the University of Alberta in Canada in the summer of 2016, she implored the young graduates in the audience not to become a victim of Imposter Syndrome. She talked about her own experience of turning up at Cambridge as an undergraduate in the 1960s, feeling overawed and immediately anxious about her lack of cleverness.

'I knew they'd made a mistake admitting me. I knew they were going to throw me out sooner or later. But I decided in the interim I would work my very hardest, so that when they threw me out, I wouldn't have a guilty conscience. I'd know I'd done my best. And so I was being very diligent, very thorough, very conscientious, following up every anomaly that our new radio telescope turned up. And that's what led to the discovery of pulsars.'[31]

This diligent and conscientious hard work, fuelled by Imposter Syndrome, led to her discovering the first radio pulsars, a highly significant scientific discovery, in 1967 when she was just 24 years old.

Bell Burnell is such a star that she actually *discovered* one. Instead of paralysing her, it appears that her Imposter Syndrome motivated her to work so hard that she reached great heights. If you can't immediately change the voice inside your head, perhaps there's a way to use it as fuel that propels you to do great things.

FIVE SLOW NOTES TO SELF ....

1. Imposter Syndrome is a big fat liar.

▷ Look at the research. Pauline Clance's website (www. paulineroseclance.com) is a powerful resource of studies and information on Imposter Syndrome, and a worthwhile place to allow yourself a spell of productive procrastination.

▷ Look at the evidence of your life and your achievements to date. Take some flipping credit, will you?!

▷ Use the fear of Imposter Syndrome to spur you on to do great things, rather than let it paralyse you. Think of Bell Burnell and her star.

2. Comparison is the thief of joy.

▷ Be careful in your use of social media and how you are comparing yourself to the carefully coiffured feeds of others. Think about what you put up online in comparison to what your daily life is actually like. Online and offline, 'compare and despair' is a fiendishly clever contributor to feelings of Imposter Syndrome.

3. Get to know your Inner Critic. Give them a name if that helps.

▷ Normalise and externalise your Inner Critic by creating a character, like my Aunt Linda, inspired by Kristen Wiig's *Saturday Night Live* character of the same name.

▷ Try to give your Inner Champion a name, too. I'm still working on mine, but 'Dolly' – as in Dolly Parton – is a definite contender.

▷ Only say to yourself what you would say to others.

▷ Remember that a thought is just a thought. It's not necessarily the truth.

4. Perfectionists: learn to settle for Good Enough.

▷ Our brains may be programmed, in an evolutionary sense, to seek out the negative, but be mindful not to give too much weight to negative feedback.

▷ Perfection does not exist. If you are a perfectionist, it will make a huge difference in your life to finally, fully and truly accept that there is no such thing as perfect, and that your idea of Good Enough is probably about as close to perfection as you're going to get.

5. Get some notions about yourself, for feck's sake.

▷ Life is short; give yourself a break. Be proud of what you have achieved, and try not to rely so heavily on the praise of others to bolster your self-esteem. Try to allow positive praise the same amount of attention as negative feedback. But be cognisant of the power praise has over you and be mindful of how it motivates you.

SLOW READS ....

Some long reads on the art of getting to know your Inner Critic and how to embrace your very human and utterly perfect imperfections.

• *How To Be An Imperfectionist: The New Way to Self-Acceptance, Fearless Living, and Freedom from Perfectionism* by Stephen Guise

- *Playing Big: Practical Wisdom for Women Who Want to Speak Up, Create and Lead* by Tara Mohr

- *Embracing Your Inner Critic: Turning Self-Criticism Into A Creative Asset* by Hal and Sirda Stone

THREE

Gut

Whether you want to call it your intuition, your inner voice or a sixth sense, having a direct line to your gut can help you make decisions that have your best interests at heart. So how do we set up these lines of communication between our head, our heart and our gut?

I'm pretty sure my gut speaks Dutch. For the longest time, this meant my gut and I had serious communication issues. I had no idea what it was telling me and I didn't care enough to listen or to learn its language. When it tried to speak up, I ignored it in favour of what external pressures were telling me to do, or what my head or heart wanted.

Apart from the language barrier, my gut has a quiet speaking voice. Even though her ideas are solid, she has struggled to be heard. There's such a competing cacophony of opportunities, obligations, fears and possibilities that her good advice gets drowned out in the noise. I've had to learn to take the time to give my gut some space and let her speak.

To figure out how to better understand my gut instincts, I consulted *mBraining: Using Your Multiple Brains to do Cool Stuff*, by Marvin Oka and Grant Soosalu. Oka and Soosalu developed a suite of methods called mBIT (Multiple Brain Integration Techniques), based on leading-edge research in neurosciences, to learn how to work with our three brains. That's right. According to the neuroscience that underpins Oka and Soosalu's work, we each have three brains; our enteric (gut) brain, our cardiac (heart) brain and our cephalic (head) brain.[32]

Traditional folk wisdom tells us to follow our heart and our gut while also telling us to use our head. 'What are we supposed to do with all this apparently contradictory advice?' Oka and Soosalu ask. 'Our answer is: "do them all."'

According to Oka and Soosalu, our gut brain is primal and it developed, both evolutionarily and in the womb, before the heart and the head brains. 'It [the enteric, gut brain] is the intelligence that is at the core of your deepest sense of self, your subconscious sense of who you are and who you are not. It's also the intelligence that is at work dealing with all core identity based issues and motivations such as needs for safety, protection, maintaining boundaries, and what you will physically or psychologically internalize or reject.'

'A lot of our thoughts and processes are driven by what's going on in our gut,' Dr John Cryan, neuroscientist at the APC Microbiome Institute in the University of Cork, tells me. Dr Cryan and his colleagues have been involved in groundbreaking research into how gut health influences our state of mind and brain function. Their research looks into how the microbiome, the ecosystem of good bacteria that have been living in your gut since birth, impacts aspects of the physiology of humans. One of Dr Cryan's interests is interoception. 'It sounds like a Christopher Nolan movie,' he tells me. 'But it is how we feel and sense what is going on in our body. That sense is driven from our gut. We have clear signal pathways that govern the choices we make. Subconsciously can we sense what's going on in our gut? It's at the interception of neuroscience, psychology and philosophy.'

Oka and Soosalu make a clear distinction between the main functions of our three brains: the head brain's prime functions are cognitive perception, thinking and making meaning; the gut brain is concerned with mobilisation, self-preservation and core identity; while the heart brain's functions include emoting and values. This breakdown is a useful starting point from which to translate the messages you're getting from your head, heart and gut. If you can figure out where a message is coming from, that might make it easier to decipher what the messenger is trying to tell you.

FOLLOWING YOUR GUT TO CREATE BOUNDARIES

What are boundaries? How can we instil them into our work lives? What do they have to do with our gut? And why are the most well-intentioned self-imposed boundaries so fecking easy to break?

'To me, good boundaries at work comes back to having a stronger sense of self,' the organisational psychologist and life coach Leisha McGrath tells me. 'A stronger sense of self is a connection to your gut. If you can hone in on what your core values are, it will help you to create the boundaries that you need to make work work for you.'

The Fumbally Café is one of the most creative businesses in Dublin. It was founded by friends Aisling Rogerson and Luca D'Alfonso, who took over the abandoned shell of a post-Celtic-Tiger office building in 2012 and transformed it into a home for simple yet extraordinary cooking. There's a giant sign on the wall with a quote from *Don Quixote*: 'All troubles are less with bread.' It's a social space, meeting space and a space for inspirational food.

The Stables, an 18th-century building next door to the café, houses their 'exploratory taste lab', where they test out their own pickles and fermented foods from kombuchas to kefirs to vinegars. The shelves in the test kitchen are filled with jars of fizzing, burping and bubbling live foods. The Fumbally team host classes on fermented and pickled foods, sharing what they've learned about the connection between fermented foods and a healthy gut. They don't do social media, and it turns out they don't have to. They're busy all day every day, and their food does its own advertising for them.

In the summer of 2015, a letter was pinned to the front door of the café and shared on the café's website. 'Do you know when things start to become slightly overwhelming ... you realise that you have been continuously adding things to your life but you haven't taken anything away to balance it out? ' read the note. 'That's kind of where we're at ... It has become apparent that for us to continue to give the service that we want to give in The Fumbally we need to make some space. We need to not grow any bigger in terms of staff and we need to all have the energy to be able to arrive into work happy and fresh. This is why we have decided to close on Mondays.'

Wow, I thought to myself when I saw it. Now those are some good boundaries.

The letter in full was soon shared online by customers, some sharing it alongside their only half-joking despair. 'Noooo! Where will I get my sunflower seed milk flat white on a Mondayyyy?' On the whole, the decision was warmly supported by customers and admired by others in the food industry.

'Honestly, it had an initially negative impact financially for us,' Aisling Rogerson told me. 'But less than a year after we decided to close on Mondays, the financial side of it levelled out. Most importantly, it has given us the space for what we intended. We've used the extra time to experiment more in The Stables and to develop it as an events space with a learning programme, as well as launching our Wednesday dinners in The Fumbally.'

Setting those boundaries and reclaiming time gave The Fumbally team the space to nourish their creativity. Rather than working less, they were working smarter. They weren't taking a day off, they were reclaiming a day for their own pursuits so that their work could be better every other day. It also gave them space to make sure their values were all lined up, nice and neat in a delicious, fermented row.

You might not be in a position to reclaim an entire day for your own future planning, creative pursuits or skill development. But could you cordon off an hour or two a week to check in with your values? Do you have the choice to carve out some time and put up boundaries to make sure your time isn't wasted by others or, perhaps more likely, by yourself? If you have the capacity to carve out that time, are you able to follow through by putting up boundaries around that time to protect it from others or yourself?

Marriage equality boundaries

At Body & Soul Festival in June 2015, I spotted Andrew Hyland sunning himself on the grass with a friend in the middle of the festivities. I went up to say hello. 'I just wanted to thank you for what you have done for Ireland and for my family,' I said. I knelt down next to him, put a hand on his shoulder and I started to cry. 'Oh, Aoife, you're welcome. And I'm really sorry,' he said as he started to laugh. 'This is just too funny. I was literally just telling my friend here that people keep coming up to me and crying. And here you are!'

The reason Andrew Hyland kept being confronted by criers is because, as co-director of the marriage equality campaign, and as a founding member and Director of Communications for Yes Equality, he played a central role in Ireland's groundbreaking Yes vote on marriage equality on 22 May 2015.

Nearly two years to the day after that referendum, I sat across from Andrew on his sofa and spoke to him about boundaries. How had he been able to sustain himself and work on what was a deeply personal campaign? Where did the job end and Andrew begin?

'Pretty much from the moment I could walk, I was bullied for being gay,' he explains. 'But I came from a family of activists so I had a natural urge to fight against injustices.' After his early life as a target for bullies, Andrew engaged in some deep therapy in his 20s, working through his demons. In his 30s he found yoga and meditation.

By the time the campaign rolled around in the lead-up to the referendum, Andrew knew who he was. He was proud of who he was. So when opponents to marriage equality spouted bigoted propaganda against the LGBTQ community, Andrew just knew it simply wasn't true. He had already worked through that type of bullying in therapy and knew how to protect himself. He was able to set aside the personal so that he could focus on the political.

In October 2014, Andrew went to Bali for an intense two-week yoga and meditation retreat. When he got back to Ireland, he hit the ground running and didn't stop until the week after the successful Yes campaign. He set up a strong set of boundaries to help himself get through this period. 'I did it by saying No a lot,' he says. Kind of ironic for such a high-profile Yes campaigner.

He moved into an apartment by himself, so that he could leave at 6 am in the morning without disturbing anyone and then come home, late at night, and not have to talk any more. He had no TV so he would sit on the sofa and simply not speak. He allowed his family to help him by doing his washing and cooking his food. When things got tough, he tapped into the top-up of inner peace he had gotten at the meditation retreat back in October.

Not only did his strong sense of self and his boundaries support him through the campaign, the crucial piece of the puzzle was that he knew the extreme pace of it wasn't going to be for ever. 'The reason I could sustain this momentum was because I had a very clear goal – a Yes vote – but also because marriage equality had an end date: 22nd of May 2015. One of my favourite yoga teachers, James Higgins, asks, "Is your practice sustainable – and can you apply that question to your own life?" That's an important question that I ask myself a lot.'

What did Andrew do next? He's now a Community Relations Manager on the Public Policy Team at Google. He sets boundaries between his work and life, and brought his learning about the importance of his meditation and yoga practice to his current role. 'Marriage Equality was a once in a lifetime job. Actually, it was a vocation.'

The power of no

It feels good to say yes. It's positive. It's seizing the moment. It's grabbing life by the goolies. It's what our western culture – heavily influenced by the status placed on work by our cousins in the USA – has brought us up to do. Just do it!

It's hard to say no, whether you work in a corporate environment or for yourself. There's a shared fear in both scenarios. If you say no, you won't get ahead. If you push back, they'll ask someone else the next time. People who work for themselves, particularly at the beginning of their career, can have an almost pathological fear of saying no. My inability and fear about saying no contributed to my Big Burnout of 2015.

I've been re-training myself in the art of saying no to the wrong things so that I can say yes to the right things. Saying no to a draining work project so that I have room to take on a project that will help me grow and make me feel good. Can I use my head, gut and heart to help me say no?

'"No" is really powerful,' Clare Mulvany tells me. Mulvany has previously been a photographer, yoga teacher, writer, blogger and coach. She co-ran Trailblaze, an Irish-based 'Ted Talks with soul'. She is currently a life coach and founder of the creative coaching programme Thrive School. She told me: 'No becomes more powerful when there's a bigger yes calling – saying no to smaller things so you can make space for a bigger yes. When you have that bigger yes, a dream, a vision, or a project when your yes is clear, then your nos are much easier. If we understand our values, we can develop a set of criteria around saying no. Tuning in to your gut instinct is linked to values. Your gut intrinsically knows what is good for you.'

Life coach Leisha McGrath agrees. 'I think we need to say no more. I think the default is yes. When we're saying yes, we need to fully understand what we're saying yes to. We don't really think about what it means if we take on that piece of work or that deadline. Very often, a little bit of gentle push-back can buy you an extra week with very little consequence on the other side. So why put ourselves under this relentless pressure all the time? Sometimes just asking the question, "Would it be ok if I gave it to you on Wednesday instead of Monday?" will mean that you won't be working on the weekend.'

Saying no may be all well and good for self-employed people who have the choice and the control to say no. What if you work in an office for a demanding, unapproachable boss? What if you work in a caring profession where people's health relies on your availability? How can you say no?

Kim Keating is a Senior Clinical Psychologist in one of Ireland's largest children's hospitals. In her work at the hospital she has to be flexible with her boundaries. She might start the day with a planned schedule of patients to see, but her day could change in an instant with the arrival of unexpected or emergency consultations. 'It's kind of like surfing a wave,' she told me. 'You can be pulled from every direction and you have to be very flexible. That can be at a cost to you personally if you're not used to it. There's always pressure to do everything, and do everything really well, but everyone has a different capacity and approach to managing things.'

Being aware of the external pressures, like the expectation and value put on saying yes to everything and being helpful, is a good start, says Keating. 'In a way, in the psychology profession, you do have permission to say no, because we see the importance of having to look after ourselves. If we don't look after ourselves, we can't look after our patients. We try to bring into our awareness the external pressures and how we're reacting to them through monthly individual and peer group supervision sessions.'

What does it feel like to say no at work? Is it easy? 'For me, I try and do what I can at work. I also know that there are times when I can't. It will cause me a bit of discomfort to say no and create a boundary. It can be really hard if you can't do something for a patient you have developed a really good relationship with. You can't do everything for other people and you can't even do everything for yourself.'

Keating uses coffee breaks as a simple marker of whether she is letting her work take over and is saying yes to too many things. In her previous job, coffee breaks were hugely valued. They were never missed. When she first started in her current role, her colleagues used to joke with her that she was obsessed with coffee breaks, but for Keating it was a really simple way of setting up a boundary around work and her own wellbeing. 'I can tell when my boundaries are out of whack if I didn't get my coffee break in a day or as is often the case a few days in a row.'

Using a non-negotiable break, even if it doesn't happen at the same time every day, as a small way of saying no means that you can carve out the time necessary to say a more important yes.

In June 2017, an out-of-office email sent by Madalyn Parker, web developer at Olark, a live chat company in Michigan, went viral. It notified her colleagues and contacts that she was taking two days off to look after her mental health. It wasn't just what her out-of-office message said, but also her CEO's response that made the headlines. 'I just wanted to personally thank you for sending emails like this,' wrote the CEO, Ben Congleton. 'Every time you do, I use it as a reminder of the importance of using sick days for mental health – I can't believe this is not standard practice at all organisations. You are an example to us all, and help cut through the stigma so we can all bring our whole selves to work.'[33]

Granted, you may not have a CEO as sympathetic as Congleton. His response is an example to CEOs and managers everywhere, particularly in his recognition of the importance of bringing our 'whole selves' to work and that the occasional, well-thought-out 'no' can actually make us better at work in the long run.

While working on this book, I became braver about saying no to projects which I knew would deplete me of the energy I needed to write. But I must admit it was still the kind of bravery that had a wobbly foundation. After saying no, I would feel the fear: 'Will they ever call again? Will I make enough money for the rent next month?' Saying no still feels a bit scary to me, but I am building up a reserve of courage that is rooted in my open line of communication with my gut.

It takes courage to say no. It also takes an understanding that we have the right to say no, and that sometimes saying no is essential to enhancing our capacity to do our job well.

HOW TO FOLLOW YOUR GUT INSTINCT TO MAKE CHANGE

Suppose we check in on our values and realise that what we want isn't quite lined up with what we're doing. How can our gut help us to change that?

The 1989 classic business manual and self-help book, *The 7 Habits of Highly Effective People* is basically the business equivalent of Michael Jackson's *Thriller*. It has sold millions of copies, inspired other great work and it's constantly referenced. Despite its biz-speak title, it's a really good read, even for those outside the business world. Its author, Stephen R Covey, wrote: 'The key to the ability to change is a changeless sense of who you are, what you are about and what you value.'[34]

We often associate change with something drastic. Moving country. Quitting our jobs. But real change is a slow process. Perhaps never-ending. 'Change is the constant,' says the creative coach Clare Mulvany. 'Every single moment is in flux. Even as you're speaking, you're nodding, you're blinking, you're breathing, the light is changing, the noises around us are changing. Change is life.'

Pivoting

'What does my head say? What does my heart say? What does my gut say?' Jenny Blake is the author of *Pivot*, a book she wrote after leaving her job as a Career Development Program Manager at Google in Silicon Valley. She's now an international speaker, career and business strategist and executive coach, using her *Pivot* method to help people create change in their work and lives.

'Sometimes what our head, our heart and our gut are saying to us can become conflated and unclear,' she tells me. 'The head is what we *think* we should do, our heart tells us what we *want* to do, and the gut is kind of like a referee between the two,' she says, referencing Oka and Soosalu's *mBraining* book. 'I think it is really important to separate your intuition and gut feelings from fear. It can be really hard to make change if your inner voice is clouded by the fear of "What will happen if ...?"' Blake recommends acknowledging the need to change to oneself, quietly and privately. Sometimes admitting to yourself that you need to make a change will get the ball rolling, even if you need to sit with the decision for a while before acting on it.

In other words, your gut 'will communicate with you when big decisions are on the line, if you pay attention to it, and it will sound alarms when your most primal needs are not being met. The process of working with it is like building a muscle – it takes time and practice. Start by examining big decisions you have made in the past, noting when and how your gut communicates with you in the present.'

THE VALUES OF THE HEART

In a 2014 article on Huffington Post, author and work coach Anne Loehr makes the distinction between ethics (or morals) and values. They're different. 'Values are what is important to us, what we "value" and what gives us purpose.'[35] Loehr suggests that most of us have between five and seven core values. As we know from *mBraining*, values are the domain of the heart brain.

Whether you respond to the Oprah-esque language of chasing your destiny or prefer the down-to-earth vibes of following your gut, if you take a closer look you'll realise they are just two ways of saying the same thing. Find the words that feel the most comfortable to you and start hunting for your values or taking a self-led class in the language of your gut.

Figuring out your values takes an investment of time, and the process of finding them will be different for each of us. The investment of time might mean an hour alone in a coffee shop with a notebook and a list of common values (just do an online search for 'values' and you'll get a list – then choose the values that resonate for you). Your list might include words like community, creativity, craic, generosity and fairness. Hey, check it out, those are five of my core values!

When I catch up with the American writer and women's rights activist Jamia Wilson, we are just three months into the Trump presidency. The bigotry, misogyny and chaos that his government represents is keeping me awake at night on the other side of the Atlantic. So what must it be like for Nasty Women on the ground in the US?

Wilson campaigned at grassroots level for Hillary Clinton, and was, like her colleagues and peers, devastated by the result of the 2016 American election. She remembers the night they realised Clinton was not going to be their president. 'I was at Hillary's election night party, where we thought the fireworks were going to go off that night,' she tells me. 'Being in the room with her family and friends, and the media who had been following her for the whole campaign, turned from one of the best moments of my life to one of the worst moments of my life, and one of the most toxic environments I've ever been in.'

After that night, she took a look inward and realised that she needed to let go of the myth of meritocracy, the idea of a society governed by people chosen according to their merit.

'Watching this person who is a charlatan reality TV star beat the most qualified person who has ever run for office in this country, on a platform based on racism, sexism, xenophobia and anti-immigration, was just such a blatant reminder that meritocracy is what Americans claim to believe in but it's actually the antithesis of how things get done and how power gets distributed. In order for me to move on and be effective, I needed to shed my commitment to perpetuating that myth myself. On a personal level, I believed that if I worked twice as hard I could defy these systems, but that's not actually true. I still believe in accountability and working hard but I really needed to stop believing that work was going to set me free, especially working in a way that would deplete me and my community, and leave me exhausted. I'd been conditioned to buy into the idea that work will set me free.

'In the beginning, I felt like I had to be at every single rally, write every single Op-Ed, call up every single tweet ... but actually that doesn't create life force. There is a limited amount of life force that each of us gets. Every nanosecond, there is something happening that is worthy of outrage, and that expends so much energy. So now I feel like, yes I need to show up and be accountable, but I need to be intentional about when I'm there, and when it's ok for me to step out to recharge and rejuvenate, and let someone else carry that weight.

'When I see Trump is away playing golf, and see all this vacation time he's taking ... I actually think it's kind of wise. Even though I think it's hugely problematic and hypocritical, given how he criticised Obama for doing the same thing, he's actually taking his time to rejuvenate, recharge and recalibrate while the rest of us are spinning.

'It's so destructive that just because there isn't a system support for them that other people should be denied time off. I think a lot of that comes from collective trauma, and people wanting some reason for why they suffered. At the end of the day it doesn't help anybody.'

Just like Andrew Hyland in the build-up to Ireland's referendum, in the wake of the US elections Jamia set up boundaries for herself, creating a system to help her process and prioritise the work that comes in. She asks herself four things when a request or a project comes in:

▷ Does it remove any current obstacles – physical, spiritual, work or health?

▷ Does it help me achieve my goals?

> ▷ Does it help me get free financially and make a living through my strength, my voice and my skills?
> ▷ Does it help me and the people I love stay healthy and thrive?

'I don't always adhere to the questions, but it really helps me get rid of the guilt of saying no to being pulled into something that isn't nourishing to me, or that doesn't tick those boxes,' she says. Instead of saying yes, she has also started to use her strengths of connection and delegation, passing on work to someone who has the capacity and whose priorities are aligned with the project. Sometimes where she draws a boundary creates an opportunity for someone else. She continues:

'The learning that brought me to this point was so important. I know what it looks like to work yourself into numbing oblivion. I know that it is actually not a good long-term strategy. It keeps you from doing the work that you should be doing and it keeps you from clarity, so I am really trying to be long-term and strategic about it. The difference now is that I am more deliberate and calculated about how I use my time. This is my strategy to stay in the game longer.'

It took a critical blow to a cause that Jamia had believed in her whole life (meritocracy) for her to question just how much she was giving of herself, and to create that space between 'react' and 'act'. While we may not all be working on the US elections, I think we've all probably hit rock bottom at some point, only to realise that the way we are working *isn't working*.

Which of Jamia's questions could you ask yourself, when you know you're overwhelmed and being pulled in too many directions? Have you hit rock bottom before – and if so, what did you realise to be true at that time? How can you stay more in touch with yourself and your boundaries so that it doesn't take such drastic measures to make you slow down in future?

What are your values?

When I look back on my trickiest, ickiest, most stressful times at work, I can see now that at my lowest points my values were way out of whack. Whether the project I'm working on isn't aligned with my core values (community, creativity and craic), or the people I'm working with don't share my values, when there is a conflict between what I *want* to do and what I am *actually* doing it can cause a lot of stress. Particularly if you aren't aware of your values, or don't know where your gut lives – or your gut speaks Dutch.

In a café in Blackrock, Dublin, I sat down with Leisha McGrath for an hour of values talk. She is a work and organisational psychologist and life coach based in Dublin.

'In coaching, I'm not giving people the answers,' she explains.
'I'm simply asking them questions and allowing them to tease
out what they already know. You guide them to look in and
uncover what's authentic to them, and ask them questions
like, "What do *you* want?" As my yoga teacher says, if you like
it, do it, if you don't like it, don't do it. But a lot of us are trying
to please other people, or we're worried about what other
people think of us.'

The business psychologist Johanna Fullerton advises creating
space for self-reflection. She talks about seeking counsel
from people you really trust and who really know you. It's
also important, she says, to understand that sometimes the
perspective of others isn't helpful for you when making a
change.

'Realise when other people will look at the choices you're
making, they're not looking at them from the inside out.
Others may challenge or critique your changes from their
brain, but you're using your heart and gut. The languages don't
translate. To have that steeliness – to realise, "I know where
this change is coming from in me," is really important. If you
don't hold strong, it can deflect you from your change and
where you're going.'

It can be enormously useful to get a handle on exactly what your priorities are, whether to help you make the right decision now or help you start thinking about your next step. Figuring out how to distinguish between the thoughts in your head and the feelings or intuition of your heart and gut brains is a powerful step towards making decisions that benefit you and your future.

As Oka and Soosalu put it: 'The most significant and core issues that people face are due to how they are utilizing their three brains in ways that are appropriate to their outcomes.' In other words, are you tuning in to all three brains when you make a decision?

GUT WISDOM

Even if you learn how to tune into it, you might not be able to do exactly what your gut tells you.

My gut might say, 'Don't work on that project!' It might even be screaming at me to run for the hills. Whereas my rational mind will remind my gut and heart that I need the financial stability that a project will bring to my Future Self. I may have to compromise by taking on a project, but at least if I've consulted my gut, I'll walk into the project with an awareness which will in turn help me build some boundaries. Or I might decide that the finances aren't worth the potential impact on my sanity.

Making a change in your career (or your life) takes an investment in time. It's true that people impulsively decide to quit their jobs or radically alter their lives, with mixed results – some great, some not so great. Even as a generally impulsive person, I like the idea of striving for balance in making change, investing time to figure out what you really want, while avoiding going *too* slowly about it and getting stuck somewhere you really don't want to be for too long.

It's also important to remind yourself that a small change can make a big difference. 'People think change has to be really dramatic,' says Clare Mulvany. 'I'm an advocate of considering what are the little steps you can take, and also the timeframe. Change doesn't have to be for ever,' she says.

When we're stuck in the cult of busyness, we aren't listening to all three brains. We are too busy firefighting and putting out small immediate fires. We have no space to sit back and listen to our heads, hearts and guts.

As Gretchen Rubin of *The Happiness Project* says, 'Focus not on doing less or doing more but on doing what you value.'[36] That to me is a slow idea that I can get behind.

FIVE SLOW NOTES TO SELF......................

1. You have three brains.

▷ Learn how to tune into what your head, heart and gut are telling you and use all of that information to make the best decision for you right now. You have three brains. Wouldn't it be cool if you could use all of them to their full potential?

2. Use your three brains to help you create boundaries and tune in to the power of no.

▷ As Jenny Blake says, tuning in to your gut takes time and practice. When you're making a decision, try to make room for what your gut is telling you. Don't just discard a feeling of trepidation about the job because your head is telling you the money is too good to say no. Weigh up what your gut, heart and head are saying by writing out your basic reactions to a job. Find your core questions, like Jamia Wilson, and use them as a checklist when making decisions.

▷ Practise saying no to the wrong things so you can say yes to the right things.

▷ Understanding why you're making certain decisions will help you figure out if these decisions are authentic to you now, as opposed to learned behaviour that worked for you long ago.

3. Take time to figure out what your core values are.

▷ Take time out to check in on your values, either by working with a life coach or just by spending a couple of hours with a piece of paper and a pen writing notes about yourself and your life. What is important to you? What do you want? Does most of what you're doing in your day-to-day life reflect those values? If not, what can you do to change?

4. Use your new awareness of your head, heart and gut to build a stronger sense of self.

▷ If you know who are you and what you really want, you will be better able to make decisions that benefit your goals.

5. Change can be small.

▷ Remember that change doesn't have to be catastrophically enormous. It's true that small changes can have a huge impact. By simply changing how you approach decision-making by making sure you're consulting your gut, heart and head, and therefore taking your whole self into consideration, the impact on your happiness at work is likely to be huge.

SLOW READS ....

These books helped me to learn more about the connection between my gut, heart and head, as well as offering great toolkits for figuring out what my core values are.

- *mBraining: Using Your Multiple Brains To Do Cool Stuff* by Marvin Oka and Grant Soosalu

- *Pivot: The Only Move That Matters Is Your Next One* by Jenny Blake

- *The Happiness Project: Or, Why I Spent a Year Trying to Sing in the Morning, Clean My Closets, Fight Right, Read Aristotle, and Generally Have More Fun* by Gretchen Rubin

FOUR

People

There was a time when I had convinced myself I simply wasn't suited to working with other people. I was too sensitive or too stubborn, too silly or too serious. The shock that I felt when I discovered colleagues didn't have the same values as I did reverberated throughout my entire system, and the tensions of difficult working relationships kept me awake at night. I would dread criticism. I would analyse and mull over work conversations and interactions, exhausting myself with cruel thoughts of my own inadequacy. It sucked. No wonder I considered working by myself, for ever.

But then I remembered – I *love* people. I love interacting with people and finding out more about them. I love making people feel good, safe and heard. I love figuring out how other people work. An isolationist approach to working wasn't just unrealistic, it wasn't going to make me happy.

The core concepts of Stephen R Covey's *The 7 Habits of Highly Effective People* have been so widely adopted that they almost feel clichéd. On the surface, it appears to be a book about maximising win-wins and synergising. But it's actually a book about reaching your highest potential as a *person*. It's called the the habit of effective *people*, not workers, and this makes it deeply relatable beyond the boardroom.

A core theme in the book is working with others, which Covey describes as 'interdependence'. According to Covey, 'Dependent people need others to get what they want. Independent people can get what they want through their own effort. Interdependent people combine their own efforts with the efforts of others to achieve their greatest success.'

In other words, we can do well, perhaps very well, on our own, but we can do our *best* work with the support, collaboration and cooperation of others. If you've ever tried to do something completely and utterly on your own, you'll know this is true, however much you may not like to admit it. There are gaps in our strengths that can be patched up by our collaborators' strengths, and this is nothing to be ashamed of. So, in order to create our best work, I'm afraid we're all going to have to learn how to get along.

KNOWING ME

Peter F Drucker was an Austrian-born American management consultant, educator and author of *Managing Oneself*, a clever little tome that should only take an evening or two to read yet will fill you with insights about what it means to be a knowledge worker, which is a person who thinks for a living, such as software engineers, physicians, architects, design thinkers and academics. Drucker coined the term 'knowledge worker', so he was a bit ahead of his time in predicting our current predicament.

'Throughout history,' he writes, 'people had little need to know their strengths. A person was born into a position and a line of work: the peasant's son would also be a peasant; the artisan's daughter, an artisan's wife; and so on. But now people have choices. We need to know our strengths in order to know where we belong.'[37]

Drucker also recommends that knowing how we perform might even be more important than knowing our strengths. '[Knowledge workers] should know the answers to three questions: What are my strengths? How do I perform? And, what are my values? And then they can and should decide where they belong.'

The question 'How do I perform?' brings an extra layer to the traditional idea of knowing your strengths, and it's one I don't think we give enough time to. When we understand better our own flow of energy, we can really make the most of our time. Do you perform better in the morning? Do you perform well under pressure? If not, what are the circumstances that you need to perform well under pressure (for example preparation, a good night's sleep, a handy stash of emergency biscuits …)?

Do you have time, right now, to get a piece of paper and a pen and try to answer Drucker's three questions?

1)   What are my strengths?
2)   How do I perform?
3)   What are my values?

Give yourself 15 minutes. Or 30 minutes. Or the rest of the day. I don't mind if you put this book down to do it. Knowing your answers to those three questions are more important than finishing this chapter.

Knowing your weaknesses

'My only weakness is that I'm a perfectionist.' So goes the crappy old joke about the perfect job interview answer to the question of 'What are your weaknesses?' But, of course, maladaptive perfectionism really *is* a weakness. Outlining your strengths might also mean you'll be brought into contact with your weaknesses. That's OK. Knowing them will help you work with them or around them.

Among my most debilitating weaknesses are my tendency towards negative thoughts; my addiction to praise; and the unrealistic expectations I set for myself and for others. I have heaps more weaknesses, but those are the three that I've been focused on for the last couple of years, the ones that I've been unpacking (with the help of my therapist) and slowly loosening the vicious grip they once held over me.

The Salmon of Knowledge

One weekend while my friend Emily, an American academic, was visiting from Berlin, I was preparing food for a small catering job I'd been hired for. I was creating an intimate dinner for a group of 15 people. The star of the dinner table was a fish that had been caught by the party's host. He had fished a huge, beautiful salmon out of an Irish river. Caught by his own hands. On his own boat.

My job was to cook it. Totally cool, totally no pressure. Absolutely grand.

I was completely freaking out about it.

My friend Emily found me panicking in my kitchen as I was trying to transfer this enormous fish from its poaching tray to a serving dish, without snapping the beauty in two. I swore to myself that I would never *ever* take on a catering job again. 'I have *ruined* this fish. It's completely overcooked,' I said to Emily as she tried to reassure me that the fish looked good to her. I dressed the plate up with edible flowers and herbs, to disguise the culinary car crash I was responsible for.

'He caught this fish with own damned *hands*,' Aunt Linda reminded me, on a loop.

I transferred this disaster of a dish to the party venue, ready to ring Dominos for a pizza back-up as I was pretty sure that I was going to get sacked on the spot. The host saw the fish. I braced myself, ready to hang my apron up then and there. Burn the apron in fact, and never cook again.

'It looks beautiful,' he said. 'Thank you.' I relaxed a little. When the time came for the guests to actually eat the fish, my anxiety spiked again. As they tucked in, I spied on the party from my position in the kitchen and caught the host's eye. He nodded in appreciation. He was happy. I hadn't destroyed his fish. It wasn't in the slightest overcooked. I looked at the fish again and could finally see that indeed it did look beautiful.

'Have you ever heard of cognitive distortions?' Emily said, when I went back home and told her that I had actually done a good job of cooking that fish.

The theory of cognitive distortions is one the foundation ideas of cognitive behavioural therapy (CBT). These exaggerated thought patterns can wear us down to the point of anxiety and depression. Thanks to my friend Emily, I started reading about this theory and the work of psychiatrist Aaron T Beck, popularised by David D Burns in his 1980 book *Feeling Good: The New Mood Therapy.*[38] Having a basic awareness of some of the key themes has helped me to put in place a thought-checking process.

Some common cognitive distortions are:

▷ Mind-reading, where you think you know what people are thinking about you (and it usually ain't good);

▷ Catastrophising, when you blow up a problem so much that you are waiting for tragedy or disaster to strike;

▷ Internal control fallacies, when you think you are responsible for the happiness or unhappiness of everyone around you; and

▷ Labelling, where instead of thinking 'I made a mistake' you think 'I'm an idiot' or 'I'm a loser'.

This is just one theory about identifying negative thought patterns, and one that I've found helpful in soothing my own negative thought patterns, which are the thoughts that Aunt Linda thrives on. Being aware of these distortions has helped me to become more aware of when my thoughts are 'alternative facts'. I've started to approach my thoughts as an investigative journalist might. Looking for evidence and trusted sources to decide whether what I'm thinking is true. When I find myself thinking, 'She thinks I'm an idiot,' I can usually catch it now and ask myself, 'Do you have any real *proof* of what this person thinks or are you mind-reading?'

If you have a look online for Burns' checklist of cognitive distortions, you'll find a list of some of the other common cognitive distortions. You might notice that you have a habit of indulging in one, a couple or almost all of the distortions. If you notice a lot of your behaviour in this theory, perhaps it might be an idea to explore CBT as a method of helping you slow down this part of your thought patterns. Sometimes, a little bit of self-awareness is enough to stop the mind from tumbling into a negative thought spiral.

I HAVE TO PRAISE YOU, YOU HAVE TO PRAISE ME

In a *Harvard Business Review* IdeaCast interview, the author Tara Mohr speaks about questioning our reliance on praise. She recommends we ask ourselves, 'Is my relationship with praise really serving my biggest goals?' She explains:

'What I find is that for many people, they come to a juncture in their careers where, to move forward, they need to evolve their relationship to praise, particularly if you've been a high achiever. And that could start early in your life or early in school. Or it might start when you really found your groove in your career. And you're used to getting gold stars. And you're used to getting awesome performance reviews. And you're used to wowing the client. And you're used to getting the job that you applied for. All those kinds of things I would say are forms of praise. And we can become reliant on that, and addicted to that.'

My generation and the young ones coming up behind us have been raised on a deliciously sweet and sugary diet of praise. Trophies. Stickers. Ribbons. Incentives at school followed by incentives at work. We're propelled by extrinsic motivation, the type of motivation that is built on external rewards, incentives and praise. In the book *Punished by Rewards: The Trouble*

with Gold Stars, Incentive Plans, A's, Praise and Other Bribes,
author Alfie Kohn looks at the long-term impact of being too
generous with praise, whether it's teachers in schools, parents
at home or bosses in the workplace.

Kohn drew on hundreds of studies to argue that the work
people do when they're being motivated by bribes such
as praise is inferior to the work they do when galvanised
by the purer motivation of doing the work for the sake of
achievement. Kohn advocates for parents, teachers and
managers to 'move beyond the use of carrots or sticks.'[39]
His work is often mentioned when it comes to reports of
millennials being praise addicts in the workplace, which their
Baby Boomer bosses have a hard time relating to.

I am a praise addict in recovery. Sometimes, after a Sing Along
Social show, I would catch myself *actively* seeking out praise
from the crowd, but in a very understated and nonchalant way.
I would simply walk through the crowd, pretending to myself
to be on the way to the bathroom or the bar (even though
I don't drink, like, who am I fooling?), and I would smile at
people and soak up their compliments on the show, to be
stored in my self-esteem battery pack.

Extrinsic motivation isn't all bad. But would making room
for more intrinsic motivation, doing something because it

feels good for you and not because you have an audience to please, help direct you away from an unhealthy appetite for praise? If I can accept that the Sing Along Social is worthy and valuable and enjoyable for me, will that mean praise-hunting won't have the same sense of urgency? That it could just be for fun? Can I actually give *myself* what I've been looking for in other people – namely love, acceptance and approval?

My friend Paul Brennan is a mountain climber in his spare time. He once showed me a photo of his sleeping arrangement on the side of El Capitan rock formation in Yosemite National Park. It was a sort of covered hammock, a death trap sleeping-bag to my eyes, that he had somehow attached to the side of the mountain at a height of 650 metres. It was utterly terrifying. He loved it. Even as an amateur climber, he could relate to the idea of an addiction to praise.

'Climbing at its worst can be a negative circle of praise- and approval-seeking,' he told me. 'My experience is that the social currency and praise you get from putting yourself at risk can lead to people seeking out risk just to get more praise, particularly when your sense of self-worth is low.'

Praise-seeking can be a prison. If you're constantly searching for it, you might even end up hurting yourself trying to feed your hunger for it. 'There are other reasons to put yourself at risk that can be extremely fulfilling,' Paul explained. 'In my experience, the positive reasons come from internal motivations, the negative largely from external motivations such as the need for praise and glory.'

Should we really be so focused on what other people might think of us, anyway? Do we even know for sure what others think? Are other people even thinking about us? As Guise says in *How to Be an Imperfectionist*, 'If you think people expect perfection from you, take comfort in the fact that most people don't care what you do.' Taking a step back and reminding yourself that that you're not actually the centre of the universe can be strangely reassuring.

KNOWING ME AS A BOSS

People who drink coffee in Ireland have a lot to thank Colin Harmon for. He's the founder and CEO of 3fe, a specialty coffee shop and roastery that has had a huge influence on how Irish people drink coffee. He's also author of *What I Know About Coffee Shops*, a great read for any self-starter looking to set up their own business inside or outside the coffee club. He launched 3fe in 2008 from a small counter in the front hall of a Dublin nightclub during the day, before the flat white had arrived on our shores.

Harmon went through a bit of a transformation as a boss. His company grew quickly, from one employee (himself) to 40, in less than ten years. He had to figure out along the way how to manage people.

When Harmon reached a point that was close to burnout a few years ago, he realised he hadn't been delegating as much as he could have been. Not only did it mean that Harmon was being stretched too thin, it also meant that his staff weren't getting enough of a sense of ownership at the company. 'If I was coming in at the last minute and finishing off a project for someone, not only was I taking it over from them but I was also getting all of the praise.' Harmon had to take an honest look at that behaviour and realise it was really demotivating for his team.

Harmon's wife, Yvonne Scanlon, is an occupational therapist, and because of her work he had an added awareness of how his team were feeling at work. 'We have a really dedicated team,' he says. 'If I come to the café and the vibe is really great, the coffee is great and the food is great, I'm really appreciative that my team create this when I'm not even there. I owe them a debt of gratitude to make sure their environment is the best possible. People told me when I got into this that the worst thing about running your own business is managing people. But I think it's the best part. It's the most rewarding part and the most difficult part.'

Alongside his Executive Head Chef, Hilary O'Hagan Brennan, who is also a co-founder of the Athrú conference which focuses on women's equality in the food industry, he has developed a wellness programme for his staff. It's made up of a regular meeting that is open to all but voluntary to attend, to give staff a chance to share parts of the working experience that aren't working for them. The team try to implement ideas from those meetings, such as the creation of a small meditation room in their busy Grand Canal Street café. This is a little escape pod for staff to go into when they're feeling a little stretched by the day's work.

Harmon had to own up to his own failings in order to create a better place to work. That can't have been an easy thing to do but 3fe is now an example of how small businesses can work with their team members to keep the lines of communication open regarding how people are feeling at work.

In a *Harvard Business Review* article, Anthony K Tjan, co-author of *Heart, Smarts, Guts and Luck: What It Takes to Be an Entrepreneur and Build a Great Business*, explained his belief that you can't be a good leader without self-awareness. 'By giving us a better understanding of who we are,' writes Tjan, 'self-awareness lets us better understand what we need most from other people, to complement our own deficiencies in leadership.'[40]

What if you think it will show weakness to admit your failings as a boss? 'The only person who is educated,' wrote Carl R Rogers in his 1961 classic book on the self, *On Becoming a Person*, 'is the one who has learned how to learn and change.'[41] By recognising your failings, and figuring out how your crew can help you plug those blindspots in your capabilities as captain, you're actually creating a much stronger, better, safer ship.

PRESENT ME VS FUTURE ME

Sometimes I think Present Aoife just doesn't give a hoot about Future Aoife. As far as Present Aoife is concerned, Future Aoife must be superhuman. I mean, if she isn't, then why does Present Aoife keep taking on more and more work for Future Aoife? Does Present Aoife actually care at all about Future Aoife's mental wellbeing? The jury is out.

When agreeing to workload or obligations, it's important to connect with your Future Self so that you can say yes or no

accordingly. Otherwise, certainly in the case of a time optimist
(or time delusionist is probably more accurate) like myself,
your Present Self will completely overwhelm your Future Self,
either by taking on too much or letting the instant gratification
monkey take over, leading to procrastination paralysis.

Dan Goldstein is a Principal Researcher at Microsoft Research
who studies online economic behaviour and decision-making.
In a Ted Talk entitled 'The battle between your present and
future self', he used the old story of Odysseus asking his first
mate to tie him to his ship's mast to avoid the temptation
of the Sirens' song. 'Tying yourself to a mast is perhaps
the oldest written example of what psychologists call a
commitment device,' says Goldstein. He goes on to explain
that commitment devices are things like not having junk food
in your house if you're trying to lose weight, or locking up your
credit card in a drawer with a key. He also notes how easy it
is to ignore these self-set commitment devices and to 'weasel
our way out of them.[42]

'The other reason it's difficult to resist temptation is because
it's an unequal battle between the Present Self and the Future
Self. I mean, let's face it, the Present Self is present. It's in
control. It's in power right now. It has these strong, heroic arms
that can lift doughnuts into your mouth. And the Future Self
is not even around. It's off in the future. It's weak. It doesn't

even have a lawyer present. There's nobody to stick up for the Future Self. And so the Present Self can trounce all over its dreams.'

This disconnect between the actions of the person we are now and the implications of the person we will be in the future causes fierce trouble at work. Have you ever agreed to give a presentation about an upcoming project on the same morning as your deadline for a current project? When you initially said yes, your Present Self had total confidence in your Future Self. 'She's got this,' you said to yourself without understanding that you will eventually become that Future Self ... and by scheduling two high-pressure situations on the same morning, you have just put your Future Self (i.e. YOU) under quite a bit of stress. Why is it so difficult for us to recognise that our decisions now impact our Future Selves? Harvard psychologist Daniel Gilbert believes it's because we simply can't imagine that our Future Selves might have different needs from us. We think who we are now is who we will always be. 'Human beings are works in progress who mistakenly think they're finished,' says Gilbert in a Ted Talk entitled 'The Psychology of the Future Self'. 'The person you are right now is as transient, as fleeting and as temporary as all the people you've ever been. The one constant in our life is change.' [43]

The benefits of connecting to our Future Selves are obvious. Studies have shown that people who are more connected with their Future Selves make better financial decisions[44] and feel more in control of their lives.[45]

Let's take Gilbert's reassurance that the one constant in our life is change. We can change the way we connect with our Future Self, and it's something many of us naturally do as we grow older. We are more mindful of the risk of taking on too many extra-curricular or personal commitments around peak times at work. Through experience, we learn what works and what doesn't work for our continuously changing Future Self.

A good place to start, I think, is consulting your Future Self when making decisions about your future. After all, it's your Future Self who will be impacted by these decisions made in the present. Simply ask yourself, 'What will my Future Self think about this decision? Will they go bananas when they realise how much work I've taken on for them? Or have they got this?'

Making it a regular practice to consult your Future Self on decisions that directly impact them might help you to make better decisions, so that by the time Present Self becomes Future Self, you really *have* got this.

CONSTANT CHANGE

Getting to know yourself in a more detailed, intimate way can be a tough process – we might not always like what we find. Discovering unhealthy or ugly patterns in our own behaviour, like a tendency to be passive-aggressive when stressed or an inability to delegate, can be hard truths to swallow. But you have to recognise these patterns and tendencies before you are able to change them in yourself.

Talk therapy has been the most successful route for me to get to know myself. Having another person to help you catch your patterns is invaluable, because it's so hard to do it on your own. Meditation and mindfulness have helped me with this, too, as they have helped me to learn how to be with my own thoughts without trying to fight them or without them taking control of the wheel too much.

I've actually started to like myself a bit, warts and all. Even Aunt Linda has become softer, more forgiving and more accepting of my shortcomings. As Rogers puts it, 'The curious paradox is that when I accept myself just as I am, then I can change.'

KNOWING YOU

Consider this truth bomb from *The 7 Habits of Highly Effective People*: 'Valuing the differences is the essence of synergy – the mental, the emotional, the psychological differences between people. And the key to valuing those differences is to realise that all people see the world, not as it is, but as they are.'

It takes some of us longer than others to realise that not everyone thinks the same way as you. Many of us naturally surround ourselves with people whose views reflect ours and who share our beliefs, loves and hates. Not because we actively want to live in an echo chamber but because it's fun hanging out with people who laugh at the same things as you and reassuring when they cry at the same things. As the old saying goes, you can choose your friends but you (usually) can't choose your work colleagues.

That's how that saying goes, right?

At any rate, a lack of understanding of differences in the workplace can lead to a lot of unnecessary stress.

Personality types

People are complex creatures. It's unhelpful and reductive to box people into strict categories. But I would argue that there is value in applying the idea of personality models as a guide to help understand differences at work. There may be a sniff of dystopian creepiness in massive organisations asking you to take a personality test (which, particularly the Meyers-Briggs, are not without controversy). But in practice, understanding differences is a huge part of teamwork, and understanding our personalities can be a stepping stone towards that.

My sister, Niamh, is part of the Learning & Development Team at Google in San Francisco, and she has used personality tests when working with teams. 'People are like icebergs, and our personalities are the very tip of that iceberg,' Niamh tells me. 'Personality Type Indicators are a window into preference. They can give a team of people a shared vocabulary and a level playing field for difference. The first step is self-awareness and the second step is self-regulation.'

Whether it's by taking personality tests or by taking time to grow in self-awareness, understanding what makes you and your colleagues tick is a vital ingredient in healthy teamwork. Being open to understanding other people's perspectives can help ease the frustration you may feel about a colleague you just don't *get*. 'Seek first to understand, then to be understood' is another central tenet of Covey's work.

R.E.S.P.E.C.T.

Muriel and Kevin Thornton are a bit of a dream team. They've been a team for more than 25 years, in life and in business. While Kevin worked in the kitchen at their Michelin-starred Dublin restaurant Thornton's, Muriel led the front of house team, right up until the couple decided to close it in 2016.

They have gone through a lot together, from surviving toxic kitchen cultures (not in their restaurant but in others), to navigating the chef shortage crisis currently plaguing the restaurant industry around the world, to losing their two Michelin stars in the space of five years (much to the bafflement and dismay of the Irish food community).

Throughout it all they have remained side by side, a solid team, true partners. Where Kevin is the creative force, the one who headed off to the west of Ireland in the middle of the night to dive for scallops to serve in his restaurant later that day, Muriel is the organiser who takes care of the emails, the schedules, the team and the front of house. I met them for a chat about what it's like to work together as a couple.

What is clear is that Muriel and Kevin really, really respect each other. They respect their differences and they use each other's strengths to make their own work better. 'We have huge respect for each other,' says Muriel. 'We push each other and

125

we are 100% honest with each other, but at the end of the day we don't cross the line into each other's work.' They were strict about their rule of not talking about work on a Sunday, when the restaurant was closed, and they were dedicated to spending that time with their children instead.

'Collaboration' is a word that's been hijacked, like 'values' and 'innovation'. It's been sucked into meaningless corporate marketing speak, though it is actually so important in our everyday working lives. Perhaps particularly for freelancers or business owners, finding the right collaborators is essential to a happy, productive working life.

A business partnership is like a marriage – it's wise to not jump straight into it before you really, *really* know the other person. Sometimes people get lucky when they jump in, but other times they don't. It doesn't have to be as dramatic as finding out that your collaborators are dishonest or selfish. Rather, it can be as simple but potentially destructive as discovering that your core values are out of whack. In the best-case scenario, your strengths are complemented by your collaborators' strengths, and vice versa.

TOXIC WORK CULTURES

It's not just working kitchens that foster toxic environments, but it is a profession that is known to have harboured a culture of negativity in the workplace. 'If you were an accountant, and you walked into work and your boss called you a four-letter word, there'd be a tribunal,' says Colin Harmon of 3fe. 'I've had chefs who've worked for me who talk in glowing terms about how a head chef threw a bowl at the back of their head.'

The restaurant industry is a good case study of toxic workplaces, and it's a subject that leading chefs have been increasingly speaking out against over the last five years. René Redzepi, the pioneering chef at Copenhagen's Noma, considered one of the best restaurants in the world, wrote an article for *Lucky Peach* magazine about the culture of the kitchen, outlining how he had learned to cook while being screamed at by his superiors, so he just naturally brought that into his own kitchen. 'I've been a bully for a large part of my career,' Redzepi admits in the piece. 'I've yelled and pushed people. I've been a terrible boss at times … When we started trying to change the culture at Noma, we did it for the sake of our own happiness. I didn't expect that it would also make us a better restaurant. But it did.'[46]

It's not easy for a boss to admit they've acted badly or to realise their employees feel bullied by them, but it's the responsibility of the leaders of industry to detox their workplaces. Otherwise, employees have little choice but to follow their example or eventually move on.

Annika Fogarty is a counselling psychologist and executive coach who specialises in cognitive behavioural therapy and mindfulness therapy. She notes that an organisation's culture can breed the conditions for burnout. 'If you're in an unhealthy, toxic work environment, this can contribute to burnout. Staying late in the office is contagious, for example,' she says. 'There is a huge onus on management to set realistic expectations and healthy boundaries at work.'

Toxic work environments can sometimes creep up on us. It can take a while to identify the bully or the manipulator among our colleagues and it can be a shock when they appear. If you think you might be experiencing workplace bullying, consult someone in your workplace HR department or someone you trust in a management position to get their advice on how to deal with the issue. If your place of work is less formal or you work as a freelancer, there are some useful resources online that might help you to look at the issue objectively and figure out how to cope with it.

DIFFERENT VALUES

It can cause shockwaves, frustration or even anger when

you discover that your close business partner or collaborator doesn't share an identical set of values to you. You might realise that your value of community actually isn't that important to your collaborator, who places higher value on an intense attention to detail, for example. Maybe you value fun and inspiration, where someone else values order and discipline. Depending on the circumstances, neither of you is wrong, right?

People don't have identical sets of values. Somewhere along the way, even with someone who seems to be completely and totally on your wavelength, you are going to care about or prioritise different things. Rather than focusing on those differences, what's more important is being in touch with your own values and also being aware of how much you're willing to compromise on those. How far is too far out of your comfort zone? How can you use your values as a compass at work?

'Sonder' is a word created by the American writer John Koenig for his online project *The Dictionary of Obscure Sorrows*, and he defines it as the 'realisation that each random passerby is living a life as vivid and complex as your own'.[47] Isn't that a beautiful concept? If you can apply it to the people around you at work as well as the random passerby, it may give you the space to understand that each and every one of us is having our own experience, with its own set of problems, values, successes, failures, triggers and joys. Most of us are doing our very best to manage it all. Perhaps the idea of sonder can help give us some empathy when it comes to dealing with others in the workplace.

It's also important to remember that the people you're working with are not Michelle Obama. Being aware of having unrealistic expectations of colleagues, collaborators and co-workers is as important as realising that you have unrealistic expectations for yourself. Not everyone cares about the same things as you, and people will put varying degrees of effort, love, blood, sweat and tears into things that you might think are really important. Having a good dose of self-awareness about what you are expecting from others may help you to soothe some of the tension or frustration of certain work relationships.

It's rare to find a job where you can avoid working with others. Even solitary writers have editors they must consult. Librarians have research students. Truck drivers have route managers. It's quite difficult to avoid some sort of cooperation, so if you find work relationships tricky, sessions with a talk therapist or life coach might help you unpack what triggers you about working with others, and how you can learn to work in a way that's good for you and for those around you.

Besides, it's by working with other people that opportunities are created. Sometimes it takes other people to see your value and to take a chance on you. They see potential in you that you can't. For example, my editor took a chance on me by commissioning this book. Anyone who's hired me for a project has taken a chance on me. It's important to work well with others because of the opportunities they can create for you, as well as those you in turn can create for them.

A slow perspective

The Venerable Panchen Ötrul Rinpoche has lived and trained as a monk since he was four years old. In the 1980s he was sent to the UK by the Dalai Lama on a mission to set up an inter-faith dialogue. In 1990, he was asked by Irish students of Buddhism to become the Spiritual Director of Jampa Ling, a newly established Buddhist Centre in the wilds of Co Cavan.

I visited him there, to prepare for an intimate but public interview I would be conducting with him a few weeks later in Galway. 'I've got about ten questions for Rinpoche,' I said to myself as I drove through leafy Virginia. 'That should give us enough to talk about.'

Fast-forward to the last five minutes of my allocated interview time with Rinpoche and his translator and nephew, Younam. We were still on question one. Even though we'd been talking for nearly an hour. 'I've *got* to get him to talk faster and get through these questions,' I thought to myself, feeling anxious that I wasn't going to get the quote I needed for my book.

And then I realised how silly I was being. 'Aoife, are you *actually* trying to rush an elderly Buddhist monk to get to the point about how to be slow in life?!'

I took a deep breath and relaxed, and brought my attention back to the present moment and the monk who sat before me. And then, just as we were about to wrap up the interview, Rinpoche told me about how he felt towards the Chinese prison guards who had captured him in the late 1950s.

When Rinpoche was four years old, he was identified by Buddhist monks as a reincarnated honoured Buddhist teacher. In 1959, when he was still in his teens, the Chinese came into Tibet and started imprisoning Buddhist monks in an effort to quash the religion. He and many of his fellow monks were captured. He was kept in a labour camp for a whole year, doing 14, 16 and sometimes 24 hours of manual labour a day. Finally he and two of his friends escaped, and they travelled under the cover of night through the Himalayan mountains to freedom in India.

It took Rinpoche a whole hour to tell me that part of his story. As I was getting up to leave, he gave me this nugget of wisdom. 'I want you to know that I feel really grateful to those Chinese prison guards.' When I asked him why he said it was because he was really physically strong after that time in the labour camps. If it hadn't been for all that physical work, he never would have been strong enough to make the journey through the Himalayas.

Got my quote! But I was also reminded of three important lessons:

1) You can't control what others do to you but you can control how you react to them.

2) If you're hoping to learn something from someone, you should be prepared to be patient.

3) You can't rush a Buddhist monk.

As Covey puts it, 'It's not what happens to us, but our response to what happens to us that hurts us.' Rinpoche's story is an extreme one. Here's hoping your boss doesn't make you run for the hills of the Himalayas to escape under the cover of night. But it is important to realise that, though you can't control or change others, you absolutely *can* control how their actions impact on you.

FIVE SLOW NOTES TO SELF..........................

1. Take time to grow in self-awareness and learn who you are.

▷ Learn who you are, how you perform, and what your strengths, weaknesses and values are. Explore your inner self with a therapist or do some self-led study by reading Carl R Rogers' *On Becoming A Person*.

2. Introduce your Present Self to your Future Self.

▷ You have *got* to get these two talking. Your Present Self will start making better decisions if they realise they are the same person as your Future Self.

3. Learn about who you are around others.

▷ Pay attention to how the behaviour of others affects you. Are you taking criticism too personally?
▷ Be mindful of misleading thinking, like cognitive distortions such as mind-reading and catastrophising.
▷ Remember that you can't control how people act but you can control how you react to them.

4. Remember that we are all different, and that's not a bad thing.

▷ We don't all share the same values. Rather than feeling

disappointed when people don't share your values, focus on how their values are actually enriching your end goals at work. That's the beauty of collaboration – we each bring our own set of skills and values to make a project better than the sum of its parts.

5. Be aware of toxic work cultures and don't be afraid to ask for help.

▷ Toxic work cultures can have a catastrophic impact on our happiness and health. Reach out for help, whether it's from a family member or friend, or a trusted colleague in an HR or management position at work, to figure out the best way to cope with the situation.

SLOW READS ....

These books offer outlines and roadmaps to who we are at our core as well as who we are at work.

- *The 7 Habits of Highly Effective People* by Stephen R Covey

- *Managing Oneself* by Peter F Drucker

- *On Becoming A Person: A Therapist's View of Psychotherapy* by Carl R Rogers

FIVE

Burnout

I've sunk into the corner of my sofa. It's twilight but to find the energy to reach over and switch on the lamp feels utterly impossible. I feel like my body is broken. My inner spark, the pilot light of my being, has run out of fuel. There are no ideas left. No space for joy or craic. Only a tearful exhaustion lives here. I've been running on empty, pushing myself through deadline after deadline, working too many jobs while carrying the burden of Aunt Linda (my Inner Critic) on my back and leaving no room for recovery time.

This is beyond tired. This is burnout territory.

But what is burnout? How do we get there, and how do we get out of there?

►-◊-◄

Anecdotally, you and I both know that burnout is prevalent. If you're reading this book, it's likely you've experienced it, perhaps multiple times. Worldwide, studies have been collecting data on the epidemic of burnout, such as one in the US which found that 95% of Human Resources leaders see burnout as a major problem at work, and point to it as a cause of high turnover of employees.[48]

'What we refer to as burnout today is what used to be more commonly known as a nervous breakdown,' Fiona Brennan, a hypnotherapist who specialises in the subconscious, tells me. 'What most people mean when they say burnout, is actually the *process* of burning out. You haven't come to a complete stop yet but you are like a piece of frayed thread holding everything together. Close to breaking point. That's where we need to focus our attention, so that we can prevent a complete burnout.'

Apart from common signs like exhaustion, insomnia, anxiety and depression, Brennan notes that an early sign of burnout is when a person becomes ill as soon as they go on holiday. 'The body has taken over. The body already knows you are burning out.' I don't know about you, but that idea of being sick on the first couple of days of a holiday has become part of the vacation itinerary for myself and my peers. It's the norm to have pushed yourself so hard that your first day of rest feels more like the first opportunity for collapse. Maybe we shouldn't be normalising that so much.

Similarly, Johanna Fullerton, business psychologist, compares our work culture to a situation where we're moving so fast, we don't even have time to ask ourselves why we're running. 'A trend we've noticed is an "always on" culture and a "work hard" culture,' she tells me. 'One of the challenges for people is not even *realising* they don't have enough recovery time. It's almost like a hamster wheel where they're running hard and fast and they're dedicated, but they haven't even taken enough space to ask themselves if they should be on this hamster wheel.'

I have been that wrecked hamster, spinning plates and pies, running as fast as I can, trying to keep up, going round and round in circles on that wheel. I *really* don't want to be that wrecked hamster anymore.

THE CULT OF BUSYNESS

Perhaps one of the reasons it's so easy to remain on that hamster wheel is that everyone else around us seems to be on the hamster wheel, too. Are we running to keep up with everyone else? And just when did the word 'busy' become an adjective to describe our emotional wellbeing? Consider this:

'How are you?'

Deep exaggerated inhale 'I'm *busy*. How are you? Busy?'

Equally dramatic exhale 'Yeah, *so* busy.'

How many times have you had this conversation, or something along the lines of it, with a friend or work pal?

As an experiment, I did my best to forget the word 'busy' and temporarily remove it from my vocabulary bank while I was working on this book. When people asked me if I was 'busy' I would reply, 'No, I'm trying not to take on too much this year,' or 'I'm working on lots of fun stuff and I'm doing good.' The answer was so off-script in the cult of busyness that people would sometimes do a visible double take when I said I wasn't 'busy'.

In a piece for *Image* magazine about 'burnout syndrome', the writer and magazine publisher Roisín Agnew wrote, 'The use of "stressed" as a suitable replacement for "fine" in answer to questions about your wellbeing seems to have given linguistic licence to be openly and permanently sick in public.'[49]

Are we stuck in a cult of busyness? When did being busy

become such a status symbol? Is there any real value in the pang of pride one gets when sending a pre-7 am email (I just had to get up super super early because I'm *so* busy)? Does busyness equal success?

The cult of busyness and the macho element of boasting about how busy we are is not a new idea. Back in 1985, the *New York Times* high-society lifestyle columnist Barbara Ehrenreich penned a witty rebuttal against the 'cult of conspicuous busyness'. Ehrenreich argues that those who are truly successful are not 'the kind of people who keep glancing shiftily at their watches or making small lists entitled "To Do".

'The secret of the truly successful ... is that they learned very early in life how not to be busy. They saw through that adage, repeated to me so often in childhood, that anything worth doing is worth doing well. The truth is, many things are worth doing only in the most slovenly, half-hearted fashion possible, and many other things are not worth doing at all.'[50]

With our busyness status updates ('How are you? Busy?') we continuously perpetuate the notion that busyness equals success. 'It's incredibly easy to get caught up in an activity trap, in the busyness of life, to work harder and harder at climbing the ladder of success only to discover it's leaning against the wrong wall,' writes Covey in *The 7 Habits of Highly Effective*

People. 'It is possible to be busy – very busy – without being very effective.'

Let's just drink in that statement. You can be busy without being effective. Busyness does not equal efficiency. It doesn't even equal success, does it?

Does success really mean you are up at 6 am, answering emails by 7 am, juggling eight projects, half of which you don't even enjoy or like, grabbing lunch at your desk, not having time for your friends and family, or for your health, and multi-tasking until you feel like you are suffocating under the pressure and stress of everything you have taken on? Is that really the only version of success we can visualise?

Anyone who has been caught up in the myth of multi-tasking has felt the pain of inefficient busyness, otherwise known as 'flustered flapping about'. As a woman, there is a misconception that I will be naturally good at holding 20 pies in the air while juggling a small baby elephant. I can tell you from personal experience that I can only do one thing very, very well at a time. Maybe two. But that's it. I mean, I *can* do ten things at the same time, sure, but not at the quality I hold myself to.

In *The Organized Mind: Thinking Straight in the Age of Information Overload*, the award-winning cognitive psychologist Daniel J Levitin unmasks the myth of multi-tasking as a neural impossibility. 'Our brains do have the ability to process the information we take in, but at a cost. We can have trouble separating the trivial from the important and the processing makes us tired.'[51]

I was reared on multi-tasking. My parents had four children and two, sometimes three jobs each throughout my childhood. They were masters of multi-tasking, by necessity. In that environment, I became quite 'good' at multi-tasking, or so I thought. For a lot of my school and early working life, I did a lot of things, all the time, but none of them very, very well. Jack of all trades and master of none. I've been working hard to consciously unlearn that behaviour, and stop myself falling into the trap of ineffective multi-tasking. The generation of women before me were told they could have it all, but my generation and the generation below me have discovered, painfully, that trying to have it all is just too much pressure. I might want to have it all, but I simply can't. If I do less, I can enjoy what I'm doing more – and the quality of that activity or output is higher too.

But how do you go at your own pace when everyone around you is 'so *busy*' all the time? Won't you fall behind if you take stock and slow down? Surely you have no choice but to go at the pace of the fastest person on your team or in your office?

'It's hard to go against the social norm ... you might believe that the reason you work like you do is because of the demands upon you,' writes the business psychologist Tony Crabbe in his brilliant book *Busy: How to Thrive in a World of Too Much*.

'I would argue that this is only a small part of the picture. The quantity of work you do, and your perpetual busyness, develops because that's what everyone else is doing ... Busyness is buffet table madness. This is true in our work, it is also true in our private lives. We choose everything and end up trying to do too much. Everything isn't really a choice. In fact, what we should be doing is un-choosing things.'[52]

According to Project: Time Off, an American initiative to highlight the country's 'vacation stigma', nearly half of the employees they surveyed who were unhappy with their job or company believe it is a good thing to be seen as a 'work martyr' by their boss.[53] The idea of a work martyr is an interesting one. Colin Harmon, the boss at 3fe café and coffee roastery, recognises the macho culture around working all hours, and the boasts about working every hour you're sent. 'At this stage at my life, I boast about doing 35 hours this week. I'm proud of that. I'm trying to get that into people's minds. People will bust their ass and make it very visible. When I see people are in work until 9 pm, and they say, "Yeah, I just have to get it done," I say you must be really disorganised. I'm trying to get the heroics out of it.'

He has rejected the idea that working all the time is a sign of success. 'If you hit a 40-hour week, be proud of that. And know when you're done. If you're working 80 hours, you're not being productive. Everything past hour 50 is probably nonsense. If you can get into a 40-hour week and try to do really good work in that time, it becomes a lot more sustainable.'

'What's wrong with the norm?' writes Crabbe in *Busy*. 'There is nothing, in principle, wrong with going with the herd, if the herd is going in the right direction. In the case of busy, and responding to excess, the herd is definitely *not* going in the right direction. We need to find our own, unique responses to our challenges; we need to create a better way of doing and communicating and delivering. The answer does not lie with the herd.'

Leaning-on-the-gate time

I find myself in the middle of another kind of herd in a lush, green field in southwest Limerick, at the bottom of a hill with a fairy fort of trees atop it. I'm trying to count the cows with my friend Imen and her son Geoffrey, and figure out if the cows need to be moved to another field based on how much grass there is left for them to chew. Myself and Imen are city slickers born and bred and, though we both love nature, this is not our natural habitat.

After working in broadcast production in LA and New York City (including a stint at 30 Rockefeller Plaza), Imen settled back in her home town of Minnesota. It was there, through a mutual friend, that she met and subsequently married an Irish farmer, Richard McDonnell. She moved to his seventh-generation family farm in west Limerick and then along came Geoffrey. Their herd of dairy cows graze on the family's land in the environs of the McDonnells' home. Imen blogs about life on the farm at farmette.ie (which is also the name of her stunning cookbook celebrating Irish food). She's one half of the event production team Lens & Larder and a bit of an Instagram star.

I join Imen and her family for the kind of traditional Irish countryside daytime dinner that my grandmother used to cook, with the added zest of Imen's culinary sensibilities. There are fluffy spuds smothered in butter and flavoured with shiso, a Japanese herb that Imen grows in her garden. A ham is roasted with a smokey BBQ maple syrup served alongside steamed collard greens from Imen's garden and freshly baked bread slathered with hand-churned farmhouse butter, made by Imen from the McDonnells' herd's milk.

Work never stops for farmers. Back in April 2017, the largest farmer-owned dairy co-operative launched a stakeholder survey to address burnout in dairy farming, pointing to it as a cause of the future stifling of growth in the industry.[54] Over dinner, I ask Richard about his thoughts on farmer's burnout. Richard calls farming a vocation rather than a job. 'There is great discipline in being a farmer,' he says. 'You have to pull through the tough times and look forward to the quieter times.'

I ask him to tell me about a typical day and I'm already exhausted by the time 9.30 am rolls around on his schedule. At that time of day, he has been up for three hours and has already brought the cows in from the field for a first milking, fed the calves and checked in on his free-range chickens. If he gets to finish a day's work at 7 pm, that's considered a very good day, but he often works longer in his seven-day week, though usually Sundays are a little slower, with more time for family.

'Some types of farming are less labour intensive,' he explains, 'but when you're looking after animals, there is another level of responsibility. Spring calving season is particularly busy and sometimes you just have to work through the tiredness. It's very easy to bring burnout home with you to your family life. There's also the pressure of not wanting to be the generation to let the farm go.'

Apart from the toll on family and free time, that level of exhaustion can lead to accidents, says Richard. Indeed, the Health and Safety Authority found that the risk of a fatal injury on a dairy farm was 24 times higher than in the average workplace.[55]

Richard has been putting time into structuring and streamlining his farm over the past couple of years, changing from a twice-yearly calving season to just one. 'The farmer is so het up in keeping up with the workload and financial pressures that it can be really hard to step back and see how you could manage your time better.' That sounds familiar.

'In farming, we talk about "leaning-on-the-gate time". That's the time when you can take a pause and think about your work, and where you're going,' says Richard, and my ears prick up at the expression 'leaning on the gate'. 'It's a calm reflective time where you can put things into perspective. If you're passionate about your work, it'll always draw you in. We need more of that leaning-on-the-gate time, to plan for our future at work but also to make time for our families.'

Are you getting enough leaning-on-the-gate time? Are you getting enough time at work to reflect on what you're doing and where you're going? Or are you stuck on the hamster wheel, just multi-tasking until you drop, being busy rather than efficient?

RESILIENCE

How can a person, particularly someone who puts the needs of others before their own, protect themselves from being swallowed by the pressures, consequences and stress of their jobs?

Niall Crumlish has been General Adult Consultant Psychiatrist in a major Dublin hospital since 2010. Between administrative work, teaching, meetings and consultations, it's known as a busy job that's not very well resourced.

'It can be very easy in my job to look after other people and not look after yourself,' he tells me. 'The stresses are that it is very busy, but also that we are working with people who are in their worst crises. You are routinely in the presence of extreme suffering. It's really important to acknowledge that work can be depleting, even if it's work that you chose and that can give you nourishment. If you don't acknowledge that work can be depleting, then you will get depleted, burnt out and depressed.'

Crumlish himself has suffered from burnout and has used the concept of resilience to work his way back to good health at work. 'I think of resilience as your response to stress in your life and how you adapt and react to it. What's important to

remember is that how you respond to stress can *change*,'
Crumlish tells me. 'Resilience is about nourishing oneself.
Nourishing yourself with things like friends. You'd be amazed
by how many doctors completely lose contact with friends
because either they're at work or they're thinking about work
or they're with their young families. We can go for years
without seeing people and some of us can say "Well, that's
OK, because when we meet up it's like we've never been
apart." But, actually, that's *not* OK.

'It's about having a framework in your life within which work
exists, rather than work being the framework,' says Crumlish.
'That might sound really obvious but it's not always obvious
for a lot of people. For a lot of people, going to a match with
friends or going out for a drink happens only when work
allows time for that to happen. But these are not luxuries.
You're not indulging yourself if you do this.'

Does work fit into your life or do you try to squeeze your
life into whatever's left after work? Modern workplaces have
moved away from the traditional 9 to 5 timetable. Sure, many
of us have more flexibility at work, but instead of moving
towards Bertrand Russell's ideal of the four-hour work day, the
flexibility has meant our work hours have begun to bleed into
what would have traditionally been our free time.[56]

It's not just about the time spent at work, though. It's about the time spent *thinking* about work, too. If work is your biggest focus, your main priority, what you continuously put first ahead of your health and wellbeing, and that of those around you, then your framework is out of whack and needs some readjustments to enable you to be more resilient to burnout. Don't let work take over the framework of your life.

In the move away from traditional 9 to 5 roles and strict hierarchies, organisations have been known to encourage a culture of 'we'. So instead of talking about the company's achievements or milestones, it's 'We did this.' It makes a lot of sense to foster ownership and teamwork among employees by encouraging the feeling of being part of a unit, a family even. It can have genuine value for both the employer and employee. But where does the job end and the person begin?

Thanks to the gift (and curse) of connectivity, we're potentially accessible at all times of the day. On top of that, if you're an over-achieving praise hunter, you're in a prime position for getting hooked on the adrenalin of being *seen* to be at work, and most importantly being seen as successful, whatever the parameters of success might mean to you.

'If you're not able to fill your own well and be a little self-sufficient, you can become dependent and reliant on the relationships and people at work,' says organisational psychologist and life coach Leisha McGrath. 'If you don't know where the job ends and you begin, that would be an issue with boundaries, and if you don't know how to manage your boundaries, you're running on empty with a leak. How can you turn off from work? How can you replenish yourself?'

Sorcha McGrath is a play therapist for children and adults with disabilities by day and a musician in the band Ships by night. She's creative and sensitive, and has to manage boundaries carefully. 'The trick is to be flexible within your own boundaries,' McGrath tells me, 'You have to be loose with them, because being too rigid can lead to stress.'

Sometimes you just have to check your work email on a day off or even on a holiday. Sometimes that will make your life easier in the future. Sometimes, because of financial obligations, you have to say yes to a project with people you find it difficult to work with. Putting yourself under pressure to adhere to strict boundaries means you may be setting yourself up to fail and that doesn't make anyone feel better.

Life is not the same every day, and a set of boundaries that worked one day might not work on the next day. It can actually be more stressful to give yourself a hard time for checking and responding to a work email while on holiday than if you just accept that you needed to do it.

In *The Work Revolution: Freedom and Excellence For All* by Julie Clow, the author makes the distinction between True Urgency and False Urgency, and the need to stay vigilant about whether the problem you're facing in any given moment is, in fact, urgent.[57] Obviously, when faced with a truly urgent work problem, heading off for a swim in the sea is not going to go down well with anyone or help your immediate issue. But taking a moment to pause and ask yourself if this problem/email/spreadsheet can wait, and whether it would be better to take some recovery time right now, is a huge skill in avoiding the slippery slope of burnout.

This is about resilience, too. It's not just about creating a boundary between yourself and other people at work, but about creating a boundary between *you* and your work. Are you defined by what you do, or by who you are? Are you taking responsibility for how your actions now are impacting on your boundaries? Are you giving yourself enough space to rest and recover, without giving yourself a hard time for *not* chilling out? Do you resent others when they contact you, even though you have chosen to put yourself in a position of being contactable?

Nathalie Márquez Courtney is a freelance photographer and lifestyle blogger, and former editor of *Image Interiors & Living* and *Kiss* magazines. She also grew up with a travelling circus, which was owned and run by her family as they toured around Ireland. Her father was a Mexican trapeze artist and her mother was an Irish ringmaster. Their family joke is that Nathalie actually ran away *from* the circus. She was one of the first in her family to go to college to pursue a new and different career.

'What I learned from growing up in the circus is that not only does the show go on, but it *will* go on,' she says. 'It doesn't matter what catastrophe has befallen us, no matter what, come rain or shine, there absolutely *will* be a performance at 5 pm.' That familiarity with pressure meant that Nathalie became very good at navigating deadlines.

'It taught me resilience. At some point during the show, there will always be pressure. In some ways I'm drawn to pressurised environments because of my upbringing. The show had a lovely constant pulse. You always knew that as long as there is a process and people follow the process, everything will be ok.'

How did that experience translate to working at a magazine? 'I remember putting my first magazine together. I found it weirdly reassuring because you can't cancel a print run or cancel a show. The other lesson I had learned is that nobody is irreplaceable. If an act falls through, you find another one. If your clown cancels, you put someone else in make-up. You'll always find a solution to the problem. I've found that some friends have guilt or loyalty to certain jobs, like, "What would happen if I left?" Whereas I know that nothing happens when people leave. The show goes on! It has allowed me to detach when I need to.'

Work can feel like a circus sometimes. If we can give ourselves a break by knowing that the show *will* go on, that will take away some of the pressure in the now. If we are being truly authentic to our work (that is, truly doing our absolute best) then we can safely focus on the process, and the results will look after themselves.

I'M TOO BUSY TO BE MINDFUL

Shamash Alidina is a mindfulness trainer, speaker and coach who has taught meditation for nearly 20 years. He's also the author of *The Mindful Way Through Stress*. 'Stress isn't a bad thing in itself,' he said during a talk at a conference called Mind and Its Potential. 'You can distinguish between stress and pressure. A little bit of pressure is good – it gets us out of bed in the morning. Stress is only a problem when it becomes chronic.'[58]

He compares chronic stress to the difference between stretching your arm out in front of you holding a glass of water for one minute, one hour and one day. You could definitely manage the first minute, but the hour would be a bit trickier. Holding the glass out in front of you for a whole day, however, might end up with you being carted off in an ambulance. 'It's not the level of stress that is difficult for us, it's the fact that it's chronic and that it continues.'

This image of holding the glass of water becoming an excruciatingly difficult task perfectly sums up the impact of stress and burnout on a person's ability to work effectively. It's what happens when stress builds up and we become close to burnout. Because of this underlying pressure, things that were once simple for us become impossible. The energetic become fatigued. The active-minded become forgetful. The happy become anxious. The enthusiastic become detached. The friendly become irritable.

I asked Alidina more about his approach to mindfulness and how it can help prevent burnout. 'Burnout is effectively your brain's energy cutting off, and we need to find a way of reenergising ourselves,' he tells me. 'Mindfulness can allow you to put the metaphorical bags of stress down for a minute to give you a break. It's about intentionally paying attention, to focus or open your awareness, and bringing your attention to the present moment.'

As Josephine Lynch at the Mindfulness Centre in Dublin puts it, the body is always in the present but the mind is often racing ahead or looking backwards. 'Mindfulness is intentionally gathering our attention to what we are experiencing right now without ruminating on the past or asking why or worrying about the future. What mindfulness can offer is a space for us to take a breath and recognise what's happening in our body. We often don't realise the tension that we're holding in our bodies while we're focused on work. It takes intention to be mindful because the rush forward is so seductive. It's a part of our attempt to survive and get things done and get what we need.'

When I first tried to practise mindful meditation, all I could think about was that I wasn't doing it properly. It was just another reason for Aunt Linda to give out to me, this time for not being the kind of person who can just chill and relax and be zen, and all the things I so desperately wanted to be but absolutely wasn't. It was frustrating at first but I was reassured by the mindfulness teachers and meditation guides I met or listened to.

I wasn't expected to go from a crazy busy monkey-mind to Nirvana levels of zen just by closing my eyes and taking a few deep breaths. I started to relax into learning how to focus on my breath, and the more I took the perfectionist out of my meditation practice, the better I got at it. I literally *practise* meditation most mornings, just like I would practise any new skill from learning the guitar to learning how to ride a bike. I use the Headspace app and I sit comfortably and bring my attention to my breathing. Sometimes I repeat the phrase 'trust yourself' in my mind.

Some days my mind is clearer than others. Even when my mind is busy, taking five minutes to check in on that is hugely valuable. It alerts my awareness to the busyness, which is a little red flag for me to watch how I handle myself for the rest of the day. Because I've reminded myself how to focus in on my breathing and to the phrase 'trust yourself', it's kind of like that calm anchoring is in my pocket for the rest of the day, easily accessible.

You may have heard of Headspace, the app that has sessions of short guided mindfulness meditations led by former Buddhist monk Andy Puddicombe, the app's co-founder. Have you given it a go? It's really accessible and a great way to *practise* the practice of mindfulness, in the privacy of your own home or wherever you are.

Mindfulness, meditation and yoga might not be the right method for you to introduce your mind to your body. If you've really given it a good try and it's still not working for you, maybe there is another way of helping to quieten the mind. Maybe it's CBT, or maybe it's just going for a walk without your phone. Maybe it's mountain climbing, playing chess or just anything that gives you a chance to put down that glass of water that you've been holding at arm's length and carrying around with you.

'Helping people to connect the body and mind so that the mind can hear the signals the body is sending is an important part of preventing burnout,' says Fiona Brennan. 'It's really hard to be quiet, even for a minute. It's really easy to be busy.'

JAGGED LITTLE PILL

In the year that I wrote this book, I made an important personal decision. I decided, with the counsel of my doctor of nearly 10 years, to start taking a low daily dose of anti-depressants for a possibly temporary, unfixed period of time.

I had been working hard to prevent burnout in my own life for the last five years. I stopped drinking alcohol in the summer of 2013 for three months, and just never started again. I've been seeing a therapist every week for nearly that long. I eat well, mostly. I exercise, a bit. I've been learning how to meditate. I've been writing a book about slowing down at work, for goodness' sake.

Yet I was still regularly reaching crisis point. There were days when I simply couldn't get out of bed. And not in a 'You know what, I'm just going to have a duvet day with Jean-Luc Picard' kind of way. It was more of an actual inability to peel myself from my bed because of a deep dread of what lay in wait for me beyond my bedroom. The work commitments, the pressure, the pace ... and the personal problems too, outside the workspace.

Isn't it funny how you have a particular set of expectations for yourself and then a completely different set of expectations for everyone else? If a person has tried all the other options available to them and their doctor has recommended that they take anti-depressants, I would think that person has made a rational and sound choice. When it comes to my own decision to take them, at first I felt it was an admission of weakness. It's a cliché, but that feeling was there.

I also felt I didn't deserve to take them. Other people who had *really* tough things to be walking around with needed them. I have a great life! Taking anti-depressants was just indulging my whiney millennial self. In fact, it was pure notions to take anti-depressants. I didn't really need them. I should just cop on, woman up and get on with it.

But just 'getting on with it' had become really, really hard.

My experience on anti-depressants has been a positive one. It has been an extra layer of support keeping my base levels of anxiety at a manageable hum. The first week I took anti-depressants, I felt *invincible*. But it was replaced with a more authentic state of feeling generally ... good. I'm still me. I'm me on a good day, most days. I still feel stressed at times or unhappy or down, but not in the same rollercoaster spikes of up and down that I have felt for most of my adult life.

I'm not going to give anti-depressants all the credit for that, though. It's just one element of a larger wheel of me looking after myself, *really* looking after myself, for the first time in my adult life. As the deadline for this book got closer, I realised that for the first time ever, my number one priority was my mental health. My priority was no longer impressing others by excelling at work.

Because I've been so conscious of taking a little pill every day, it has motivated me to keep the other elements of my life in check. Namely:

▷ I eat a good breakfast;

▷ I'm careful to limit the intake of my beloved coffee to just two cups a day (and I might have a sneaky cup of tea on top of that if I feel the need for an extra rev of caffeine);

▷ I practise meditating for five minutes almost every morning (literally practise it – I'm still learning how to do it and my mind wanders off all the time but I am learning to anchor myself in my breath, which helps later on in the day when I can feel my mind beginning to get whipped up into a frenzy);

▷ I try to approach my work and projects with a healthy perspective, so that I can catch myself before I head into that tunnel vision of self-disregard;

▷ No matter what, I take a break by getting out to exercise, whether it's walking my dog or going for a swim in the sea; and

▷ I try to set myself up for a good night's sleep by finishing work and screen time two hours before shut-eye so that I don't head up to bed with a headful of task lists, half-formed concepts and unresolved problems.

It sounds so simple, doesn't it? Yet it has taken me five years, or 10, or 15, to get all the pieces of this puzzle together in a way that is consistent. I know how hard it is to make a change in your life, particularly when you feel so fecking *busy* all the time.

Thinking about whether I would include this information about taking anti-depressants in this book has been an interesting process. There's still a little bit of shame or discomfort in Ireland about taking medication, or at least talking about taking medication. Whether or not you would reveal you are taking any kind of medication is a personal choice. We don't all need to share. We don't all need to take anti-depressants either.

I'm not advocating for medication. Because it has been an important step on my road to figuring out how to have a more sustainable approach to work, I felt it was important to share it with you in this book. Personally, I have found it to be a positive layer of support in helping me to cope with some of my issues at work and home; to help me feel like I'm taking back control and getting off the treadmill of burnout.

FIVE SLOW NOTES TO SELF ....

1. Don't get wrapped up in the cult of busyness. Being busy doesn't equal being efficient.

▷ If you find yourself saying how busy you are with a sense of pride, you might be trapped in the cult of busyness.

Busy does not equal success. It doesn't even equal productive a lot of the time. Try focusing more on how productive you're being, rather than how busy you are.

2. Seek out some leaning-on-the-gate time.

▷ Carve out time to reflect on your work. Even if it's five minutes to contemplate what you are doing and what your next steps should be, that time to reflect, to lean on the gate and have a good think is too important not to be prioritised.

3. What is the framework of your life?

▷ Figure out if work is part of the framework of your life, or whether work is the framework that your life fits into. Work should not be the governing structure that you build your life around.

4. Embrace your capacity.

▷ Develop boundaries between your life and your work that can be flexible when necessary. Learn to distinguish between truly urgent, important and not important. Embrace your capacity.

5. Figure out what you need to feel well and develop healthy habits that support your wellbeing.

▷ Whether it's diet, exercise, sleep, a meditation practice, a hobby or medication, or all of the above, prioritise these actions because they are crucial to your ability to perform at work.

SLOW READS ....

- *Busy: How to Thrive in a World of Too Much* by Tony Crabbe

- *The Work Revolution: Freedom and Excellence For All* by Julie Clow

- *The Mindful Way Through Stress: The Proven 8-Week Path to Health, Happiness, and Well-Being* by Shamash Alidina

PART TWO

OUTSIDE

SIX

Money

On the day after St Patrick's Day 2017, I was in Smock Alley Theatre in Dublin, absorbing a series of talks hosted by Siobhán Kane under the banner of her creative collective, Young Hearts Run Free. Entitled *The Revolution Will Not Be Televised*, the theme of the talks was creativity and revolution. Among the speakers were playwright Emmet Kirwan, DJ Donal Dineen, artist Amanda Coogan, footballer Cora Staunton and comedian Alison Spittle. Oh, and me.

'Money is a religion,' said the Irish writer and economic satirist Julian Gough from the stage. 'Our system of money is a completely faith-based system. It wouldn't work if we stopped believing in it.'

Every day, we buy into the construct of money. Why am I so sure that a €50 note is worth €50? Because it says so on the note and that's what everybody else believes. You'll be swimming upstream if you try to argue otherwise. This is how our world works.

The system of consumer capitalism isn't naturally conducive to slowing down or taking one's foot off the pedal of gas-guzzling spending culture. Our mobile phones make us sitting ducks for companies whose advertising agencies carve out increasingly invasive routes to our wallets. In Ireland, yet another property bubble has created property prices in both sales and rents that exceed even those of the Celtic Tiger era, pre-economic crisis.[59] Childcare is bordering on prohibitively expensive, particularly in urban areas of the country. According to a Pobal survey of 4,300 childcare providers, the average price of full-time childcare was €167 per week between September 2015 and June 2016, with costs ranging from the cheapest of €142 in Monaghan to the most expensive of €214 in Dún Laoghaire.[60] With these basic pressures of shelter and childcare, how can we even *afford* to slow down at work?

To give you a bit of context on the kind of financial mastermind you're dealing with here, I don't own a home or any property. The most expensive thing I have ever bought is my car. I rent my house in Dublin 8 and it's looking very likely that, by the time this book is published, we will have had to move out of the city to find a home with a more affordable rent. As freelancers, buying a house isn't an option for us in the foreseeable future. Any savings I can eke out after paying Dublin's high rent rates go towards paying some modest debts I accrued in my 20s and early 30s, though I'm nearly back to a clean slate. I'm doing OK from day to day and have a modicum of disposable income but I must admit that my lack of financial security, particularly in relation to the basic need of a home, is a source of recurring stress.

There is one area of money that I'm pretty good at, however, and that is the area of slow, considered shopping. Rather than using this chapter as a sort of personal financial confessional box, or a take-down of capitalist consumerism (I'm a food writer, not an economist), the stories I've pulled together are intended to make you think a little differently about your relationship with money and how you spend it.

Before we go any further, let's just do a quick privilege check. To be able to make a choice about how to spend your money is indeed a great privilege. It requires a certain level of financial stability. Though I may not own any property or have any substantial savings to speak of, I'm doing just fine from day to day. I can afford at least one trip abroad a year. I regularly splurge on fancy crackers and cheese. I'm mindful that those stuck in the vicious cycle of poverty and scarcity don't have the choice to slow down with money. But I am also one of the many Irish people who can't afford to buy their own home. So, surely, I need to just get on with the rat race and work every hour I can get and save so that I can buy a house somewhere I don't want to live? Or do I have another choice?

Is there such a thing as slow economics? What would it look like to give up money? Do we need to keep earning more and more to keep up with the demands of what we 'need' to buy, or can we be happier with less? If we took a close look at our relationship with money, would it influence how we spent it? Of all the things that we buy, what do we actually need?

THE MONEYLESS MAN

I'm driving through the wilds of Knockmoyle, near Loughrea in Co Galway. The Slieve Aughty Bog spreads itself out across either side of the road as I drive around looking for the Moneyless Man. I'm lost. I don't have directions to where I'm going and it's not on Google Maps.

I finally see a house on the road. A gaggle of country dogs bark in welcome and in warning at me as I get out of the car. Their owner, his friendly face weather-beaten, walks over to me from his back shed to see what I need. He knows who I'm looking for and where I need to go. 'You're looking for the free pub is it?' He draws me a map and I jump in the car to get back on the right track. 'Good woman yourself, good woman,' he says enthusiastically, as if he's never seen the likes of a woman driving around on her own looking for a man living without money.

I follow my new friend's neatly drawn map. I turn onto a small, windy, hilly road. I pass houses, slowing down at each one to look for clues. Is this the place? And then I see it. The Happy Pig free pub, just about recognisable from the photos in the article I read about this crowd-funded project. There's a small country house to the front of the property. The door is wide open and there is a large, old brass bell hanging outside the front door. I give it a dong and a man appears. 'I'm looking for Mark,' I say. 'I'm kind of a pen-pal of his.'

I go beyond the house, past the Happy Pig pub, down a narrow path that leads me over a small, narrow bridge over a stream. Finally, through a clearing in the trees, I see a small, neatly painted wooden cabin. To the back there's a very healthy garden of raised beds, sprouting with food.

I knock on the door of the cabin and wait. And then the door opens and there he is.

Mark Boyle. The Moneyless Man.

On 24 November 2008, the activist and writer Mark Boyle embarked on a year- long experiment of living without money. Boyle, originally from Donegal in Ireland but living in Bristol in the UK, had been working towards going off the grid since his early 20s, and had previously founded the online Freeconomy movement. He captured the challenges of living without money in a book called *The Moneyless Man: A Year of Freeconomic Living*, which was published in 2010.

In the book, he describes a year living as someone who has stepped out of our money system. He lived in a caravan he got through the Freeconomy website, and parked it on a farm where he was let stay for free. In return, he worked on the farm for a certain number of hours a week. He foraged for food or accepted food from friends as long as he felt the invite would have been there anyway. He had a strict set of rules and values that he was mostly able to adhere to for the whole year.

Sounds extreme? That's what a lot of people said to Mark as he embarked on the project. 'Why, they asked, was I doing something so extreme (a word that often gets used about my way of living)? But what is "extreme"?' Mark writes in *The Moneyless Man*. 'To me, buying a plasma screen television for a couple of grand seems extreme. And given that some of the problems we will face in the future, such as climate change … are, according to many leading scientists, likely to be extreme, how can we possibly expect the solution to be moderate?'[61]

The Moneyless Man made me take a look at my own buying habits. Is everything I buy necessary? Is at least most of it necessary? 'The problem is what money has become and what it has enabled us to do. It enables us to be completely disconnected from what we consume and from the people who make the products we use.'

Nearly a decade later, and he's still living (mostly) without money outside Loughrea, Co Galway. When I look for contact details on his website (www.moneylessmanifesto.org), there's no phone number or email address. Instead, there's a note that says Mark has given up all forms of complex technology. There's a postal address, so I write him a letter telling him I liked his book and asking if I can interview him.

No sooner had I posted the note when I realised I had given him my email address and phone number as a contact. How was he supposed to get in touch with me? He doesn't have a phone or use complex technology. Would he even have stamps?!

So I wrote him another letter, this time more thoughtfully put together. It included my postal address, and I even sent a stamp, just in case.

A week or two later, a letter arrived through the post. 'It's a letter from the Moneyless Man!' I shouted excitedly to my husband, Niall. It was a note, hand-written in pencil, to say that I was welcome anytime to swing by the Happy Pig in Loughrea to see the place and say hello.

When that cabin door opened, I expected a wildling, a moneyless caveman who would growl at me for turning up on his doorstep sort-of-unannounced. Instead, I was greeted by a youthful, bearded man in an Aran-style jumper, who would not look out of place as a barista in The Fumbally Café. He introduced me to his girlfriend, Kirsty Alston, a collaborator on the Happy Pig project.

The Happy Pig is a free pub and community space, a permaculture and gift-based smallholding. People can stay for periods of time in the communal space, a small country house, which is open for people who want to explore projects that fit in with Boyle and Alston's core beliefs. The project hasn't been completely moneyless; they bought the land in Knockmoyle using funds raised through a crowd-funding campaign, as well as putting their own funds towards the project. According to a *Guardian* article in 2015, the land was part-funded by royalties from sales of *The Moneyless Man*. The site cost €95,000 and the crowd-funded campaign raised £20,000.[62] The space can have between five and 30 people living, working or visiting on the site. 'My moneyless self would probably not be too pleased about it,' Boyle said in the *Guardian* article, 'but I have moved forward and it's a means to an end that has allowed us to set up the community.'

Boyle views his lifestyle as a necessity to protect humanity and our planet, but ultimately his way of life is his choice, just as our way of life is our choice, too, if we have even a modicum of privilege. Rather than getting bogged down on whose way of living is right, what can we learn from Boyle's choices? When someone strips everything away, it can be easier to figure out what is important again without all the clutter. Though I don't want to completely give up money or technology, Boyle and Alston's lifestyle shows that at least a version of this (almost) money- and tech-free life is possible. It's a template for others who want to live differently.

As I got up to leave Boyle and Alston to their evening, I asked, 'Do you need anything?' I wondered if they needed supplies or materials for the Happy Pig, and that maybe there was someone in my network who could help, or maybe I had a skillset that could contribute to their project in some way.

He answered, simply, 'No.' It was a strikingly content and satisfied no. Mark Boyle has everything he needs right there in that little cabin and patch of land.

THE ECONOMICS OF HAPPINESS

In 2010, winners of the Nobel Prize in Economics Daniel Kahneman and Angus Deaton co-authored a study on day-to-day happiness. Their findings suggested that happiness and income are related, but only up to $75,000 per year. It's not that people become less happy when they earn above this amount, but according to their study of 450,000 survey responses, the emotional wellbeing of respondents seemed to peak at an income of $75,000 per year (nearly €69k per year).[63]

The news of this magic number made an impact. CEO at Gravity Payment, Dan Price, announced in 2015 he was implementing a flat structure of payment so that all employees would be paid $70,000, including cutting his own $1 million dollar salary to $70,000. The decision went viral. Price's brother and co-founder, Lucas Price, sued Dan for loss of earnings. Dan won the case, and the $70,000 experiment is ongoing at Gravity Payment.[64]

But to get fixated on a particular number is perhaps missing the point of Kahneman and Deaton's study. As a *Time* magazine article put it, 'when it comes to improving day-to-day emotional wellbeing, money generates diminishing returns'.[65] It's not necessarily about 'Mo' Money, Mo' Problems'. It's more that above a certain threshold, having more doesn't appear to have an impact on day-to-day happiness. What I found useful about this study is that it highlights the asset of knowing when enough is enough for you and your chosen lifestyle.

For Simon Cohen, the magic number is £30,000. Cohen is a public relations consultant and public speaker, and founder of Global Tolerance, a communications agency which specialises in non-profit organisations, charities and NGOs. His clients include the 14th Dalai Lama, the Archbishop of Canterbury and the Prince of Wales.

In 2013, Cohen put his company, including seven employees, on a one-year sabbatical, after his first daughter was born. When he returned from sabbatical, he decided to give away 95% of his shares of Global Tolerance. These shares were worth between half a million and one million pounds. Hence the headline: 'Boss of £1m firm will give it all away to be a full-time dad.'[66]

I was interested in Cohen's story and his sense of value, so I spoke to him about slowing down time through focusing on the present moment. 'When anyone loves what they do – and Global Tolerance was an extension of my heart – the very idea of boundaries would be to not honour all that I am. In my previous job, I had a professional persona, there was a boundary between my working life and my personal life, but it meant there was a boundary between who I was, which didn't work for me. I realised I couldn't have depth in focus in both Global Tolerance and my wife and daughter.

'I had an open and honest dialogue with my team about how it was going to work. There was a six-month process before we put everyone on sabbatical where we worked out the best way for everyone to do that. I wanted it to be empowering and exciting for my employees and pioneering for other companies. We had been working really hard and at a very fast pace. Everyone at the company knew that intuitively. Having an open question of "How?" worked for us.'

After that period of transition, Global Tolerance was taken over by new owners. Eventually, in 2016, Global Tolerance closed for good. Cohen is still living in Cornwall with his young family, taking on speaking engagements and working on projects he cares about. Once he has made his £30,000 for the year, he stops working so that he can spend quality time with his family.

'Even though the decision was challenging,' Cohen explained, 'it has allowed me to learn from my children, my two little buddhas, and be with them every day. I feel like the richest and luckiest man in the world. Living here in Cornwall, I didn't need to take more. I pay myself £30,000 a year and that's enough. That's not just keeping up. To me, that's thriving.'

To be able to say 'I've made enough this year' requires a certain level of income security and is a privileged position to be in. But I wonder if more of us could tap into the wisdom of the 'economics of enough'.

My friend Áine, Vice President of Legal at a leading global tech company (you may remember her from the chapter on Burnout), touched upon this topic in our chat. 'A lot of tech companies have golden handcuffs,' she told me. 'It's really easy to justify time spent away from your family because you are providing for your family.' This is such an important part of the money question. Is the money *worth* it?

'Most people think they don't have a choice because they have a mortgage to pay or whatever it might be,' Cohen told me. 'But they do have choices. If you have your basic human needs met, then you have a choice.'

MASLOW'S HIERARCHY OF NEEDS

In 1943, the American psychologist Abraham Maslow published a paper called *A Theory Of Human Motivation*, the first published appearance of the idea that became popularly known as Maslow's Hierarchy of Needs, often illustrated as a pyramid of layers.[67]

On the bottom layer, the widest, are physiological needs, which include the most basic of physical requirements such as breathing, food, water, sex and sleep. Above that is the need for safety, seen to be the security of employment, resources and property, followed by love and belonging from family and friends. The penultimate level of the pyramid is the need for esteem, characterised by self-esteem, confidence and respect by and of others. The tip of the pyramid is self-actualisation, which essentially means the need to reach your utmost potential in terms of creativity, problem solving and overall morality.

Look around you at your peers, your friends, your family, your neighbours, and, most important, yourself. Unless you live in poverty or in a war-torn country, I'm pretty sure you can identify more than one person in your network who is unnecessarily stuck on the bottom rungs of the pyramid, getting caught up with over-obtaining what they need for their physiological existence, safety and belonging, and never graduating to working on their esteem and full potential. By contrast, it may be more challenging to think about someone in your network who actually *has* made it to the top of the pyramid.

Maslow's system can provide a useful paradigm through which to look at money and how we spend it.

Food

As per Maslow's hierarchy, our physiological needs on the bottom rung of the pyramid include the essentials of food, warmth and rest.

In the Burnout chapter we met farmers Richard and Imen McDonnell. They also had something to say about the role of money in their lives. 'The farmer is a price taker, not a price *maker*. The farmer has become so squeezed by supermarkets that we're being forced to become bigger, yet the interest in farming as a job is decreasing because of the long hours and low wages,' explains Richard.

My heart sinks when I see bags of carrots or potatoes for 9c and less in the shops. Even if the supermarket chain is taking the hit on reduced prices, the devaluing of food products sets a dangerous precedent. We consumers begin to associate vegetables with unsustainable prices. Who do you think is eventually losing out? It's not the supermarkets. It's the farmers.

Innovative farmers like the McDonnells are constantly figuring out ways to streamline or find alternative sources of income; Imen and Richard are currently developing their own brand of kefir, a fermented drink, made from their herd's milk. I meet Sandra and Joe Burns at the West Waterford Food Festival in the pretty seaside town of Dungarvan, Co Waterford, at their stall for Joe's Crisps. The Burns make delicious vegetable crisps from their own-grown beetroots and parsnips. The idea of these vegetable crisps, which aren't the norm for Irish farmers, came about during the Christmas many supermarkets did a 5c vegetable campaign. It was one of the Burns' worst years ever on the farm. They knew they would have to change their business to survive.

As consumers we forget that we are in charge. I understand the pull of cheap food, particularly when you're feeding a family. Some supermarkets are better than others when it comes to the fair treatment of producers and suppliers, but it is our responsibility as consumers to be vigilant and check where our food is coming from. There has to be a middle ground where both the producer and the consumer can repair their relationship.

The middle ground for me and my income is supplementing my farmers' market shop with a conscientious supermarket shop. In a farmers' market, I can buy directly from growers like Jenny McNally at the Temple Bar Food Market or from organic importers like Christy Stapleton at the Green Door Market in Dublin 8.

Catherine Cleary, my colleague at *The Irish Times*, undertook an interesting experiment in which she shopped exclusively in local markets for seven days and then exclusively in supermarkets for the following seven days.[68] She found that her family of five only spent €11.20 more when shopping in farmers' markets. She also found that because some of the food items were more expensive at the farmers' market, such as farm fresh milk, they were less likely to waste them. There was less packaging used in the farmers' market shop, which had an impact on her recycling bin, too. She does end her piece slightly disheartened, sharing a link to a Ted Talk that convincingly argues that local shoppers are merely swimming upstream against an onslaught of supermarket power. But if it's price that's stopping you doing all your shopping locally, maybe you could do a similar experiment and see how the books add up?

Why is shopping locally and with a small producer a slow action? For me, if I meet the grower, I feel a responsibility to use that food. It not only gives me pleasure to eat food that has been grown by someone I can shake hands with, but it makes me respect the food more. I am much less likely to waste food from a small supplier, and that saves me money in the long run.

Warmth

Let's think about warmth in terms of clothing. We're faced with a problematic trend of 'fast fashion'. Cheap clothes of questionable quality and provenance, bought to be worn once or twice. Where do these clothes come from? Who is making them? Why do we need so many of them?

Triona Lillis and Aoibheann McNamara bonded over a shared love of heritage Irish materials of linen and tweed. They wanted to create a line of clothing with a modern sensibility, something that they and their friends would wear. So they created the Tweed Project. 'The Tweed Project is part of the slow fashion movement where fabric, time and craft take priority over trends and fast consumer culture,' Lillis and McNamara state on their website (www.thetweedproject.com).

Their workshop is in Aoibheann's home in Galway on the west coast of Ireland and the collection is hand-made from specially selected cuts of premium Donegal tweed and Irish linen. 'We subvert tradition,' Lillis tells me. 'It is a traditional garment. We don't want to mess with that tradition, but we want to make it modern and contemporary. It's slow fashion for that reason. It's our indigenous fabrics. They're made here in this country.

'Slow fashion is actually something very much a part of our heritage as Irish people. We have quickly sped up in Ireland but once we actually slow down and embrace what we have here, which is our indigenous fabrics of linen and tweed, there is so much more scope that people haven't really experimented with.'

Every single day I wear my Tweed Project blanket, which is most days in the colder months, I never fail to pause and think about how much I love it. I think about the women who designed it and their inspiring lives in the west of Ireland. I think about my sense of Irishness and what a precious heritage of crafts we have here. I think about Ciaran Molloy, the son who works alongside his father in the tweed weavers Molloy & Sons who make the Tweed Project blankets alongside their own stunning line of cosy blankets (without the sleeves) based on Ciaran's grandmother's design. There is a pride of place in this garment and when I wear it; that's what I feel I am celebrating. I love it when people ask me where I got it, which they often do because it is unique.

As much as I would love to, I can't afford to dress myself head to toe in the Tweed Project just yet. The blanket cost €325. Their line includes tweed aprons (€180) and crisp white 100% Irish linen shirts (€455). Not everyone can afford to shop outside Penneys, particularly if you're providing clothing for fashion-conscious children. But is there a way to curb our shopping habits? Do we really need all those clothes?

Even Lillis can't completely escape fast fashion, particularly in her work as a costume designer for Irish film and TV. 'I'm in a very happy world when I'm in a period piece where I try to do all the costumes from sourcing, finding and making, but when I work on a more contemporary TV show, I sometimes have to work completely within the fast fashion world. I've been doing costume design for 20 years. Since I started the Tweed Project in the last five years, it has really made me more aware of it. And I always bring it up in production meetings at the outset – that it is important to me to reduce waste. But it's a whole other world of fast fashion.'

It's difficult to find a high street shop with a clean bill of ethical health, but there are alternatives. Stephen O'Reilly is a full-time firefighter who shares a love for sea swimming and open water sports with his colleagues Damien Bligh and Neil McCabe, who is also the CEO at Green Plan and responsible for the carbon-neutral fire station project in Kilbarrack, Dublin.

In July 2016, they launched Grown (www.grown.ie), an ethical clothing brand designed and styled in Ireland, planting a tree for every T-shirt they produce. They are passionate about creating awareness around how fast fashion processes create unnecessary waste and negatively impact the environment. Their line of T-shirts, sweatshirts and hoodies, made from a biodegradable fibre called Tencel and 100% organic cotton, are designed to be durable as well as versatile, so that essentially their customers can maintain a minimalist approach to their closets.

'When we were out doing water sports together,' O'Reilly tells me, 'we weren't happy with the ethics behind some of the clothes we were wearing. With Grown, we hope that we can influence people and be a platform for communicating the need for change. We're really passionate about ocean awareness. Change can only be created through collaboration and community.'

When it comes to reducing waste, buying from second-hand shops means you're not adding to the clothes mountain of waste. Some friends of mine who love clothes do regular swapsies parties with their friends, to update their wardrobes in a more waste-conscious way.

At the moment, my method is to only buy clothes when I really, really have to – when the arse is falling out of my Topshop jeans, for example – and I have a look in second-hand vintage shops before going to the high street. If I'm going to a wedding, I give pause to think whether I really need an entirely new outfit. I usually don't. I invest instead in a wedding present from the Irish Design Shop.

Home

The Irish Design Shop is where I go for beautiful Irish-designed and Irish-made things. It was founded and run by Clare Grennan and Laura Caffrey, and they started as an online store before opening their first retail space in 2008. They've been in their current home of Drury Street, Dublin, since 2013.

'If slow retail means being passionate about your shop, its identity, the stock, how every item in the shop is made, the customer experience, delivering friendly service, than yes, I would say we are a slow retail shop,' Clare tells me. 'At the same time, we want to grow the business, but we want to do this without compromising on our principles.'

Their core principles are that they stock solely Irish-designed and Irish-made work, without exception. They have an 'approachable' gift-shop format so that people can interact with the products rather than feeling like they're in a gallery.

They're affordable, and a customer can always find a thoughtful, Irish-made gift for a tenner.

Clare and Laura also know the producers personally. They went to art college with a lot of the producers whose peices they stock. So when I pick up a set of geometric wooden egg cups, they can tell me about the Saturday Workshop, a father-and-daughter business that started as a way for Edward and Iseult O'Clery to hang out together on a Saturday. They'll be able to tell me about the designer who illustrated their annual calendar. Or with Clare and Laura's own stunning jewellery range, Names, I know that all of the pieces are named after important women in their lives.

To me, the Irish Design Shop, and small, thoughtful retail spaces like it, personify healthy shopping. Spending my money here as often as I can for gifts for myself and others gives me the feeling of contributing to a sustainable community chain of maker (the Saturday Workshop), broker (the Irish Design Shop) and buyer (me).

COMPULSIVE SPENDING

What if we're stuck on the bottom rung of Maslow's hierarchy because we're hooked on the buzz we get from shopping? Is our innocuous idea of retail therapy actually holding us back from facing our issues? Dr Colin O'Driscoll is a chartered counselling psychologist and addictions specialist at Change Psychology. He tells me about compulsive shopping and shopping as an addiction.

'Certain things lend themselves to addiction better than others, such as substances like drinking and smoking. Then there are three or four classic behavioural addictions, or what we call process addictions, such as gambling, pornography and sex. And the other is compulsive shopping. They lend themselves to an additive engagement because you almost get the neurological and biological experience that you get from substances. There's a high or a buzz. It can be a way of escaping from low emotions. It's a maladaptive strategy for dealing with anxiety, stress, depression or difficult relationships. It's an antidote to those feelings and it can start to become a sort of medication.

'When you use a behaviour to be OK, you can start to move towards a dependent process. Like other addictions, you develop a tolerance. You can't just buy one thing from the internet a day anymore, it's not enough. Whether or not what they're spending is beyond their resources isn't necessarily a sign of addiction, but it's a good indicator.'

If someone wanted to take a look at their relationship with

money and compulsive shopping, what kind of steps should they take to re-evaluate how they're spending?

'There's a necessity to recognise if people are over-spending,' says Dr O'Driscoll. 'It's about examining your behaviour and thinking critically about the process you're engaging in. Is it more about the purchasing than it is about the product? Do you have things in your closets that are unopened? Do you even have one or two of them? Do you have a wardrobe full of clothes that you never wear? Is this process more about your purchasing and shopping than it is about the products?'

For people who are concerned they might be over-spending, O'Driscoll recommends taking some time away from your shopping. 'Just stop. People can change. But first you need to have a personal insight that you need to make a change.'

He recommends bringing someone you trust into your confidence and telling them you're planning to cut down on shopping. If you're talking about it, that's probably giving you the best chance to make a change.

THE ECONOMICS OF SLOWING DOWN

'The reason that slow living and slow economics matter,' Dr Stephen Kinsella, Senior Lecturer in Economics at the

University of Limerick and columnist with the *Sunday Business Post* tells me, 'is because for the first time in history there are a very large percentage of people who are like you and me.'

What does he mean when he says that there are a lot of people like myself and himself? 'There is not much point in slow economics when 90% of the population has to show up and clock in,' he continues. 'But when the people who clock in have a fair bit of control over how they're going to manage their time then it does matter. I think managing yourself is a lot like managing other people. Dealing with budgets, failure, success ... these are all tasks most people didn't have to deal with before and now we sort of do. Some people faced with that task just choose to work their employee – i.e. themselves – as hard as they can. Which is kind of what capitalism has been doing for years. Essentially, you're doing the gig economy to yourself. Which is kind of crap.'

Even if you're not a freelancer like myself or an academic like Stephen, it's possible that you're a knowledge worker with some sort of autonomy over your time. It's possible that you like or even love the majority of your job. 'Having a high threshold of intrinsic motivation is actually a bit of a curse,' says Stephen. 'It means you start working long hours because you love your job so much that pretty soon you're on a path to burnout.'

It's not just the levels of intrinsic motivation that can lead us to burnout; it's the extrinsic motivation of money. A high salary. Golden handcuffs that keep us locked into jobs that have such high demands that we sacrifice our personal lives, justifying it to ourselves by the things we can provide for our loved ones by working all the time. Some are important; a secure place to live, childcare, education. Some are arguably less important; nice cars, iPads, stuff.

'If you think of our national discourse, it's about, why can't I borrow as much as I want? I want to borrow more money to buy the house. I really need to borrow half a million quid,' says Stephen. This is the mindset people looking to buy their own property have found themselves in again. My two-and-a-half-bedroom home with no garden in Dublin 8, which I currently rent, is being put on the market for over half a million euro. That is way out of my financial league.

Housing crisis aside, does Stephen buy into the economics of happiness? 'There is a certain point of income above which you don't need much money,' he says. 'But you do need to be disciplined. If you earn €100 and you spend €90, you're grand.'

So is there virtue in the idea of buying less (even if you spend a little more), and spending it locally when you do? This seems like a thoroughly slow approach, and a good ideal to try to follow where possible. 'One problem I think you have with your idea is that you are assuming that people go the same way as you go,' Stephen tells me. 'You go from cost to income, whereas most people move from income to cost. So, say I earn €40,000 a year. I will spend up to some threshold of €40,000 and I'll fill it with clothes, a nice car or whatever it is.'

He's right. I've been thinking of money from cost to income. I think about the value of what I'm buying rather than my income threshold (which might explain why I sometimes over-spend on beautifully crafted pieces of Irish design!) and I genuinely value community and provenance more than having a lot of stuff.

But I'm doing my best for the local economy by buying local in Ireland, right? 'There have been almost no studies that say investing locally in Ireland helps the local economy,' says Stephen. 'Almost no studies. The reason is that we are tiny open economy. What we're buying is kind of leaking out. It's different in America because they only export and import 10%. If you buy more stuff locally in Ireland, the chances of the person using an ingredient that isn't from here is very high. You're increasing imports of wool dye or whatever it is. There are very few things we can make here on our own ... Aran sweaters and jam maybe. We've been importing and exporting for thousands of years.'

Sigh. Why can't economics be *straightforward*?

'That local economy is certainly helpful in increasing the income of those producers and keeping them going. But whether it demonstrably benefits the local economy, there's no evidence of it. What is true, however, is that there are things you can value like sense of place, a community ritual. When we do things like this we find that people really value these places. I would imagine that even if it's not economically helpful, it's culturally and sociologically helpful. We just can't put a hard number on it.'

The approach of conscientious shopping opens up a big can of worms. Practically *everything* we buy is problematic. From the Mac I'm typing on to the cleaning products in my house, being a conscientious shopper going against the tide of the juggernaut of huge supermarket chains and worldwide consumerism means tiny, tiny wins against an avalanche of inequality and environmental consequences.

If your circumstances allow you to have even a small amount of disposable income, then the way you shop is your personal choice. But it's a choice that has serious consequences for the people you share this planet with and for the planet itself. I do my best to put my money where my heart is, as often as I can, and shop conscientiously. Even if it's just to soothe my guilty conscience of living where I live in relative luxury and freedom. That might be the only true win I can claim: that the way I shop might make me feel a little better about the inequalities of the world we live in.

Your good life

Look around and ask yourself: do we really need all this *stuff*? Do our kids need it? Can we use a slow, considerate approach to spending as a way to put less financial pressure on ourselves, and therefore less pressure at work?

'I would imagine slow economics and slow living is about figuring out how you want to live,' says Stephen Kinsella. 'What are your priorities? What is your vision of the ideal day for you? What is that? Is that working 100 hours a week as a neuroscientist? Fine. If the vision you want is working 20 hours, then 20 hours with your kids and then going for long walks, then great. What can you do to create a life that is cognisant to that vision? I'd say a lot of the work in your book is asking a very old question. What does the good life look like? And is the slow movement a way to think about the good life?'

I suggest perhaps the question should be: 'What is *your* good life?'

'That's a much better way of saying it,' he says.

Figuring out what your good life looks like is an important step towards figuring out where you can slow down in terms of the income and outcome of money. And hopefully having a really clear and intentional picture of your good life will help you find the space you need to slow down at work.

FIVE SLOW NOTES TO SELF ....

1. Identify your needs versus your wants.

▷ If your basic human needs are being met, could buying less and recognising your control over your financial choices enable you to slow down at work?

2. Experiment with doing your food shopping in local and independent shops for a week.

▷ Does it cost you much more than your usual supermarket shop?

3. Be mindful of falling into the trap of fast fashion.

▷ When you're buying clothes, can you get away from the high street towards more ethical shopping suppliers or take a look in second-hand and vintage shops?

4. Look at your shopping behaviours.

▷ Do you need to take a break from buying stuff to create space so you can evaluate why you're buying so much stuff?

5. What is your good life?

▷ Figure out what your good life looks like and what you need to do/earn/sacrifice to make that vision a reality.

SLOW READS ....

- *The Moneyless Man: A Year of Freeconomic Living* by Mark Boyle

- *A Theory of Human Motivation* by Abraham H Maslow

- *Small is Beautiful: A Study of Economics As If People Mattered* by EF Schumacher

SEVEN

Technology

Charlie Brooker is terribly clever. You may have seen his dystopian science fiction TV show *Black Mirror*. Perhaps you covered your eyes and ears to the chilling predictions Brooker made about the unintended consequences technology might have on society's future. Is the not-so-distant future of *Black Mirror* what lies ahead of us?

During an interview with (my hero) Terry Gross, Brooker was talking about the third season of *Black Mirror* and his feelings on technology. 'When I was a chain smoker, I used to wake up and the first thing I'd do was reach for a cigarette. And now I do the same thing for a smartphone, basically. I'll just automatically, without even thinking, check my phone.'[69]

This image, more than any of the brilliantly creepy predictions that Brooker had created on his show, made me think differently about my relationship with my smartphone. I can remember a time in my life when smoking in bed was ... well, kind of cool. As I've woken up to the addictive insanity of cigarettes, smoking in bed now seems beyond vile.

Yet, my brain hasn't quite made that leap when it comes to my smartphone. I mean, it's my alarm clock so it has to be in my bedroom, right?

The way we talk about smartphones, you would think that they are in control of us and not the other way around. It's far too easy to demonise smartphones and the technology that supports them, and blame them for how flippin' wrecked, stretched and frazzled we are all the time. That's not what I intend to do in this chapter. Instead, I would like you to think about your relationship with your smartphone, and I'd like to take this opportunity to take responsibility for my own relationship with my phone.

Smartphones are cool. They are an important tool in the truly incredible technology that enables us to create online communities. They can help us spread information about important things like political activism and arguably less important things like where to get the best coffee in an unfamiliar city. You can use apps to help you cook, study, learn a new language, add lovely filters to your photos and stay in touch with friends and family overseas. These are all marvellous and wondrous things.

The iPhone was launched in 2007. That's only 10 years ago. Let's have a think about that for a moment. Ten years. Most of us can remember life before smartphones, so why do we struggle to imagine life with less usage of them? If you think about it, we are only adolescents, or children even, when it comes to having this technology in our lives. Like children (and most adults, let's be fair), perhaps we haven't figured out that bingeing on something fun and cool can often change our relationship with them until we pretty much hate them.

Are we chain-scrolling? When we wake up in the morning and reach for our phones before reaching for our loved one or recognising that today is a new today, have we got a problem? How can we create boundaries around our smartphones that might help us regain a sense of control? In ten years, will we look back on our habit of checking our smartphones first thing in the morning with the same repulsion as lighting up in bed?

My dog Daffodil is a little highly strung. I think it's one of the reasons why we're such good pals – we get each other. Every once in a while, she gets a notion that there is a ball under the cushion in the sofa. She starts to scrape at the sofa with her paw, in search of the phantom ball. She gets stuck in a loop until I intervene to rescue the sofa and distract her with an actual real ball.

Around the time of the last US elections, and then again at the inauguration in early 2017, I found myself in an obsessive scrolling state on Twitter and Facebook. I woke up in the morning and scrolled through my Twitter feed, bracing myself for whatever fresh hell had happened overnight. I had breakfast, went to work (with many scrolling interruptions), made lunch, walked Daffodil, went back to work, switched on the telly to ping-pong between CNN and the BBC, all the while scrolling and refreshing and closing the app and opening the app.

I continued in this pattern for nearly a week until one night I had a nightmare that Donald Trump himself was in my room trying to get me. It was so utterly terrifying that I realised that I was just like Daffodil. My scrolling was like her scraping at the sofa, on the hunt for a phantom ball.

Are you on a futile hunt for a phantom ball? Or do you need to snap out of your smartphone habits and direct your energy elsewhere?

DIGITAL DETOXES

Daffodil had a blog for a while (daffoblog.tumblr.com), until she had the good sense to go on a digital detox. Though I respect my pooch's resistance to all things digital, the idea of long-term blanket detoxes, from food or technology, doesn't work for me. I love the potential of social media to bring communities together, though I recognise its simultaneous power of creating chasms between communities, such as the family scrolling on their devices at the dinner table instead of having an actual conversation.

Camp Grounded in California is 'where grown-ups go to unplug, get away and be free again.'[70] You're not allowed to bring children, pets, booze or drugs and the organisers provide a weekend of 'pure unadulterated fun' that includes yoga, hiking, archery, bonfires, stargazing and talent shows. The camp has a $695 price tag for a four-day getaway. Sort of like an expensive rehab for smartphone addicts. Or a restorative weekend away for an over-achiever stuck in the next-level pace of Silicon Valley work culture.

Camp Grounded and other retreats like it, whether it's a silent yoga retreat or a tech-free creative workshop, are often beyond most people's financial means. But as amazing as these retreats may be, you don't need to go to smartphone rehab to break the habit (unless you believe you might be *legitimately* addicted to technology – then you may need to see a doctor or therapist).

Take small steps towards changing your relationship with your phone. Try leaving it at home when you go out for a walk after office hours. I know! I know! The idea of that still makes me a bit anxious, too, but trust me, you can do it. I do it all the time and it means I can give all my attention to Niall (my husband) and Daffodil, rather than trailing off mid-sentence in the middle of a forest because I'm reading an 'important' email that's just come in.

I've had my notifications on my phone turned off for nearly two years now. I often take Monday afternoons off, because I usually work at the weekend. I love having Monday afternoons off. It's when my energy is at its lowest ebb. Sometimes I even (*gasp*) turn my phone off completely for the afternoon.

Once in those two years, only once, I missed an opportunity by being offline. It was an article pitch that came in from a UK newspaper, looking for me to write about Dublin's food scene. I was offline for four hours and by the time I got back to them, they had found someone else to write the piece.

The reason I missed that email is because I had taken an afternoon away from my online life. Four hours to be exact.

Initially, I was a bit bummed that I had missed this gig. I temporarily doubted my commitment to the whole 'slow' idea. But I soon realised that life and work boil down to choices. As a freelancer who works a lot of weekends, I have the luxury of choosing to take a Monday afternoon off. But by making that choice, I'll have to accept that there may be some opportunities or calls that come in while others are working. I also have to accept that I missed that opportunity and there is nothing I can do about it.

If you flip it to those who work more traditional 9 to 5 jobs, it's your choice to check your emails at the weekend. Maybe it's a good choice, one that creates less stress for you at another time of the week. But if it's not your choice, or you are feeling unfairly pressurised by your boss to do this, it's time to rethink and find out a way of pivoting the heck out of there. Or if you are finding yourself working constantly at the weekend and throughout your time off, then perhaps you need to rethink your relationship with your email.

My idea of success may be different from yours. Maybe you want to be available for those last-minute requests that come in from an internationally renowned newspaper. Maybe it would be unacceptable to you to miss out on an opportunity like this. For me, I believe that my greater long-term happiness lay in taking that time off that afternoon and accepting that I can't be on call at all times.

What works for me may not work for you. You have your own set of work circumstances that you need to figure out how to navigate. But it's about setting up boundaries that suit your circumstances, so that you feel like you're back in the driving seat. Email or answering WhatsApp messages is not your job. You've got other stuff to be doing.

EMAIL IS NOT YOUR JOB

Email is not your job, is it? Over the last decade, email has become a source of anxiety for many, pinging us with little stress darts throughout the day, interrupting our flow and contributing to a large part of noise pollution in our daily lives. We've gone through plenty of self-denial phases with it, such as the scramble to hit Inbox Zero – an approach to email management that aims to keep your inbox empty at all times. Even the designer of the Inbox Zero approach, Merlin Mann, has since moved away from the productivity space, saying 'This topic of productivity induces the *worst* kind of procrastination, because it feels like you're doing work, but I was producing stuff that had the express purpose of saying to people, "Look, come and see how to do your work, rather than doing your work!"'

According to the website of Jocelyn K Glei, author of *Unsubscribe: How To Kill Email Anxiety*, 'Email is killing our productivity. The average person checks their email 11 times per hour, processes 122 messages a day, and spends 28 percent of their total work week managing their inbox. What was once a powerful and essential tool for doing our daily work has become a near-constant source of frustration, anxiety and distraction from our work.'

Glei is not a fan of Inbox Zero and instead supports an '80/20' model. As Glei described in an interview with Monster.com, 'It's the idea that 20% of the emails you receive are going to produce 80% of the impact in the work that really matters to you. One in five emails are probably really urgent and/or deserves a handcrafted response.' Glei's key message is that 'getting over email anxiety – and being productive in this Age of Distraction – is all about learning how to set boundaries and say no'.[71]

'The contents of your inbox are setting the agenda,' writes Tony Crabbe in *Busy: How to Thrive in a World of Too Much*. 'Not because they're the right thing to focus on, but because they're in your inbox … The inputs [the emails] are not your choice; what you do, your outputs, are your choice.'[72]

I use WhatsApp for personal communications. The rolling interface suits a live chat but in my experience, it's not ideal for multi-faceted work conversations. Slack, the chat platform designed to host simplified streams of work communication, is a good example of how creating micro-boundaries can help keep things feeling ordered and controlled. Because it allows you to organise conversations into sections and folders, I use it as a complementary platform to email communications on group projects.

Though some workers have already moved beyond email, that only works if all your colleagues have given up the ghost, too. What certainly has helped me is funnelling work conversations, where possible, into two neat channels (email and Slack) and politely redirecting people who reach out about work stuff on WhatsApp or Facebook Messenger. Like any boundary, a bit of flexibility helps here, too.

PINGS OF ANXIETY: NOTIFICATIONS

'There's research out there that says every time you get an email notification and you look at it, it takes you 64 seconds to recover,' says Alex Moore, CEO of email efficiency tools suite Boomerang. 'We're living in notification hell.'[73]

I have lived through this notification hell, and it's not just the heat from email that can make it so stressful. The idea that sparked this book project came from one too many notifications coming from my phone and my laptop at the same time. It was a pressure cooker of pings, and I cracked under the building pressure of shielding myself from requests, replies, likes and retweets across a multitude of platforms.

'Clutter is not necessarily all the stuff you see around you,' Sarah Reynolds, the author and professional organiser behind the website and book *Organised*, tells me. 'Saying yes when you should be saying no is clutter. Notifications constantly coming through on your phone is clutter. These are cluttering your environment and distracting you from really focusing on your work.'

To protect yourself from the seductive sleepwalking that is scrolling through our social media feeds (literally right in the middle of writing this sentence I found myself looking at a funny picture of a cute bear on Facebook and I don't even know how it happened), create some physical space between yourself and your phone if you have to. 'I could look at my phone every 20 seconds, I really could,' says Reynolds. 'But if I leave it out of the room, I don't even think about it.'

Don't be ashamed by your apparent lack of willpower. I'm with you! I have to put my phone on the other side of the room when I'm writing. Heck, sometimes it has to be in a whole other room entirely. I put it on airplane mode overnight, so I don't fall into the trap of anxiety-fuelled 3 am chain-scrolling, and during my early morning writing sessions. The call of cute bear photos is strong!

Deep work

Those constant distractions are making it harder for your brain to focus on deep work, which was the subject of the latest book by author and Associate Professor of Computer Science at Georgetown University, Cal Newport. In *Deep Work: Rules for Focused Success in a Distracted World* he cites a 2012 study which found that the 'average knowledge worker now spends more than 60 percent of the workweek engaged in electronic communication and Internet searching.'[74]

Newport argues that as technology advances, we will be under greater pressure to 'master the art of quickly learning complicated things. This task requires deep work ... the ability to perform deep work is becoming increasingly rare at exactly the same time it is becoming increasingly valuable in our economy. As a consequence, the few who cultivate this skill, and then make it the core of their working life, will thrive.'

Newport designs his days around deep work, allowing shallow activities to be 'batched into smaller bursts' at the peripheries of his schedule. 'Three to four hours a day, five days a week, of uninterrupted and carefully directed concentration, it turns out, can produce a lot of valuable output.'

He's also an advocate for properly disconnecting from work, and he's careful to not sneak a look at his work emails or social media sites after his working day is over and he's back home with his wife and kids. 'The lack of distraction in my life tones down that background hum of nervous mental energy that seems to increasingly pervade people's lives. I'm comfortable being bored, and this can be a surprisingly rewarding skill.'

If the ability to learn complicated things quickly, which requires deep work, really does have importance for our future industries, getting into the practice of not falling prey to the temptations of shallow work (emails, updates and pings) could stand by your Future Self. For once, your Present Self could actually do something *nice* for your Future Self.

As Crabbe puts it in *Busy*, 'there is a huge difference between a deep focus on an important activity, and hopscotching busyness. It's not a quantity thing, it's a quality thing; scattered attention, doing trivial stuff rather than things that really matter is bad.'

SNAPPING BOUNDARIES

At the time of writing, Irish social media star James Kavanagh has over 30,000 likes on his Facebook page, nearly 55,000 followers on Instagram and is one of Ireland's most successful Snapchat users. I interviewed James to learn about how he managed to create boundaries between himself and his Snapchat feed.

'It's constant. My phone is a third person, and I feel like I can't ignore it,' he tells me. He tries not to be rude when out in social situations but he is online so much that people literally think there is something wrong when he doesn't update for more than a couple of hours. One time, he tells me, he was on holiday in Thailand and his phone ran out of battery. He didn't snap for almost 24 hours and people started messaging his boyfriend and his mother, Margaret, to make sure James was all right. He was fine.

At the time of our chat, Kavanagh is making his money solely from his work as a social influencer, which includes partnerships with supermarkets and wine brands. He's aware that this is a bubble that isn't going to last for ever and he's got a game plan, and that is to open a café with William. But in the meantime, he's being careful not to overdose on social media. 'I actually love social media,' he tells me, 'and because I love it so much I don't want to get sick of it.'

He's figured out that he can manage the time spent online versus the time spent offline by learning what his followers actually care about. 'I don't need to snap a whole meal from start to finish. Instead, I just do a quick snap saying something about the restaurant and something about the food, and then I can go back to enjoying my meal out with William. I've learned how to say no as well. The way I see it, sure, get your work done, but living is so much more important than work.'

This balance might seem overwhelming to some, including myself, but Kavanagh is able to sustain it because of his self-awareness. He has his eyes set on the prize and he knows that his role as a social media influencer has a sell-by date.

Cook and food writer Donal Skehan's Instagram account is followed by over 192,000 people, his Facebook page has nearly 200,000 likes, and his YouTube channel has over half a million subscribers. He is a TV host on BBC, RTÉ, Food Network and the author of seven cookbooks. It may seem frightfully tacky to reduce people to their social media stats, but it's purely to give you a sense of the type of audience Donal has. I've known Donal since our early days in food blogging, before he had even won his first Irish Bloggers

Award for Best Food Blog in 2009. Even then he had a noticeably impressive work ethic. He works *really* hard, and his commitment, as well as his output, is something he's really respected for in the food industry.

In his seventh cookbook, *Fresh: Simple, Delicious Recipes to Make You Feel Energised*, Skehan talks about his brush with burnout. He had launched himself into the world of food blogging, food photography and presenting at the age of 21 and hadn't really come up for air in that time. Three years ago, when he was only 27, his body put the brakes on for him. While working on a travel show in Vietnam, he hit a wall and ended up being briefly hospitalised. He had burnt out. It made him re-evaluate the pace he was running at and begin to create a new set of boundaries between himself and his work.

Many of us who use social media run the risk of starting to see our lives through a square panel waiting to be filtered. It's alarmingly easy for the lines between your life and praise-seeking online 'content' to become blurred. The slight rearrangement of the breakfast table spread, and the strategic cropping out of the messier part of the kitchen, mean that we're essentially curating the vision of our lives that others see. 'Social media was such a huge part of launching my career,' says Donal. 'Now we're more aware of what the perils are of social media, and the addictive side of it.'

For those who have a large number of followers or whose job is being a social media influencer, the danger of the blurring cross-over between life and content must surely be even more perilous. 'We're more conscious of the impact of social media on our day-to-day, and we're trying to make sure it doesn't define how we live our lives.'

Donal's wife, Sophie, began to make regular appearances on his TV shows. Ever since I've known Donal, Sophie has been by his side, working on his team and supporting him. They shared on social media photos of their engagement, their wedding and, more recently, the news that they're expecting their first child. These are the milestones that most of us share online these days, but is there an extra layer of pressure to share these moments with such a huge audience?

'There are things I'd prefer not to share online and so we don't. You want to keep parts of yourself to yourself. I think we do a good job in doing that, which is why when we do share things, we feel happy to do that and we don't resent sharing details of our personal lives.'

Can he take a break from his social media feeds? Or does his empire crumble while he steps away? 'Something we learned, quite early on, was that if you go offline for a month, nobody cares,' Donal says. 'Back in the early days of social media, you felt you always had to be a part of the conversation. The problem is you're feeding a beast that can never be full. Now I'm confident that I can step away from something without destroying my career. And when you actually step away from it, I've found that people are even more interested in you when you get back because you've got something new to say.

'After I reached a burnout point, I took a new approach of aiming for quality over quantity. I do my best to aim towards that, though sometimes I do ten posts a day. It's a juggling act and every single day is different. If you have the ability to switch off your phone, and go have an amazing weekend offline, and really see the value of that, that's really important.'

These stars of social media essentially work for themselves. What do their stories have in common with the office worker? The need for boundaries and a culture change is being asked for across the board, and in some cases it's being exemplified by those at the top.

'We are committed to building a better working world,' is the promise of EY (formerly Ernst & Young), the global professional services organisation. So how do they manage the energy of their own employees and build a better working world for them? I'd heard about an initiative in EY Ireland so I spoke with HR specialist Austin Hogan, whose team implemented a scheme called EY Unplugged.

'What we want to do is give people permission to switch off. Our reason for getting up in the morning and going to work, regardless of what that job is, is to deliver exceptional client service to our customers. In order to do this, we have to have flexibility in how and where our people work. We can't have a situation that we're needed and we're not there. This is not and never will be a 9 to 5 profession, but it does need some boundaries to not become 24/7. It doesn't mean we can't be responsive to our clients all over the world, but we recognise that in an age of complete connectivity we have to put boundaries up for our employees.' Particularly in a business full of high achievers, Hogan points out, team leaders have to be mindful of balance.

'One of the particular features of any hierarchical structure is that when a junior person receives an email from a senior person, there's an inclination to respond to that. We wanted to ensure that on a junior level there was no obligation to respond immediately. We have tried to put some particular boundaries around weekends and before 8 am and after 7 pm during the week.'

Hogan points out that the culture of staying late and boundaries around properly switching off on holiday also come under the umbrella of balance that EY Unplugged is trying to promote in-house.

'We want our people to switch off and recharge their batteries to enable them to be top of their game when they're here. We know from experience that if we don't do that it can be counterproductive.'

There are similar initiatives in many modern work places, and an awareness of technology boundary burnout, which is encouraging to see. To at least remind people of their choice to switch off, whether they take the invitation to do so or not, is a positive step.

Being online on holiday

Have you ever gotten a text, Facebook or WhatsApp message that says, 'I got your out-of-office email message that says you're on holiday. Can you answer a work question?' It appears the out-of-office tool may have lost its powers of protection.

For workers taking their holidays in Europe, the summer of 2017 brought with it a new perk of affordable data roaming charges, after the EU banned the practice of excessive charging for mobile calls and data downloads while abroad.

The only downside? It could potentially make it even harder for workers to switch off while on holidays.

Our access to connectivity and the pervasiveness of our emails, updates and pings bleeding into our downtime are showing no signs of slowing. Our boundaries need to be clearer than ever, with ourselves and with others. Whether you decide to actively work for a few hours while on your holidays to keep things ticking over or to turn off your data roaming and make yourself completely inaccessible, you are in control of this situation. You may not be able to control whether people contact you (even if you've given clear signs you don't want to be contacted). What you can control is your choice to respond. If you are on a *holiday*, you are entitled to that. If you do reply, then you also have to take responsibility for your part in that, instead of resenting your colleague for interrupting your holiday. They can't interrupt it if you don't let them.

It comes back to our skewed notion of what is urgent. I once considered adding a link to the dictionary definition of the word 'urgent' to my out-of-office. But that seemed a little passive-aggressive. Or maybe just aggressive-aggressive. Perhaps my most successful messaging on an out-of-office was when I shared the news that I was on a digital detox. Even if anyone had reached out to me on my other platforms,

I wouldn't have seen it, as I genuinely put away my phone for a week. It felt *really* good.

On the flip side, when you receive someone's out-of-office or a notification that they're on holiday, just think before you reach out on another platform. Is it really urgent? If it is, then thankfully we have the technology to allow you to get in touch and solve whatever emergency is on your hands. But if it isn't truly *urgent* then, for goodness' sake, let your colleague enjoy their holiday.

HOW DO YOU WRITE A LETTER?

When's the last time you sent a letter to someone? Mark Boyle, aka the Moneyless Man from the Money chapter, has turned his sights on technology these days. He has been writing a sporadic column for the *Guardian* online about living life without complex technology, which he abandoned at Christmas 2016. He writes the column by hand and posts it to the *Guardian*, and someone in their offices types it up and posts it online. It's illustrated with sketches by Boyle's partner, Kirsty Alston.

When I reached out to Mark first, you might remember that I sent him a handwritten letter asking him to contact me by phone or email if he was interested in an interview. No sooner was the card in the postbox when I realised I had to send him another card with my postal address and a spare stamp included. How was he going to phone or email me when he had given up complex technology and money? He wrote back to me in pencil. I wondered if a pen was deemed too dependent on technology in its production.

Something that is interesting about Boyle's views is the wrath that he receives from online commenters on his columns. It was the same in his columns about giving up money, which were also published in the *Guardian*. While he gets support, he gets called things like 'smug' a lot, too, or, even worse, a 'poverty tourist', based on the idea that Boyle has the luxury of leaving this lifestyle anytime he likes (or when he gets older or sick), whereas our pre-industrial ancestors didn't. I find these reactions really interesting, because they seem to be so transparently defensive on the part of the commenter.

Boyle does want everyone to stop using technology, not just because of its impact on our personal mental health and that of our immediate communities, but also the impacts of tech production on ill-treated workers in faraway places as well as the ecological impact of this industry. But we don't have to take Boyle's way of life as an insult to our own, no matter how blunt and honest he is about how he disagrees with it. Instead, my approach has been not to take offence, but to take a few notes. I'm perhaps too selfish a human to give up on the technological tools that I've built my working life around but I certainly have my ears open to the lessons shared by someone doing something differently, like Boyle. His lack of everything reminds me of the pervasiveness of our attachment to technology. The minute details of his life without technology shine a light on what many of us have started to take for granted and have forgotten about what life was like before.

Even the act of writing Boyle a letter meant I had to figure out where I was going to buy a stamp, when I was going to post the letter. I didn't know when it would reach him. The adventure of actually finding his free pub, the Happy Pig, without having any directions or a pin on Google Maps to guide me, forcing me to stop and ask a stranger for directions, was fun too.

So, write a letter to someone. Put away your phone. Buy an alarm clock. Take some time away from technology to give you some space to re-evaluate just how productive your use of technology actually is. Give yourself space to remember that you are in control of the technology, not the other way around.

FIVE SLOW NOTES TO SELF ....

1. Buy an alarm clock.

▷ Reclaim your morning by buying an alarm clock and banning your phone from your bedroom. Break the habit of chain-scrolling first thing in the morning. It's kind of gross.

2. Create boundaries around your online use, and respect the boundaries of others.

▷ Don't be ruled by your inbox and trapped into a reactive mode at work. Check your emails at particular times of the day so that you can set aside chunks of the day for deep, focused work. If it makes it easier for you to log off, check in with your colleagues and collaborators to let them know your schedule.

▷ When you're on holiday, decide how available you are going to make yourself for work enquiries. If a clear email out-of-office isn't enough – if you receive a text or Facebook message – don't be afraid to tell them you are on holiday and that you can't respond right now. Or choose to respond and take the responsibility for the choice you have made.

▷ Remember that you set your own boundaries, and it is your choice as to how fluid and flexible they are.

3. Take back control of your notifications.

▷ For me, this was turning off all notifications on all apps to limit the opportunities for allowing my phone to distract me from real, deep work. But you might not have to take such extreme action. Do a de-clutter of notifications and perhaps hold on to the ones you feel are most essential. Or you could just turn off all your notifications when you're not at work, so that work isn't seeping into your free time.

4. Be mindful of chain-scrolling.

▷ Don't get stuck in the passive activity of chain-scrolling. It's a compelling activity, but studies are now finding that it's addictive and that it makes us feel worse about ourselves, particularly when we compare our lives to the version of their lives people are sharing online. Notice when you're scrolling without purpose and break the spell by putting your phone away.

5. Be brave and leave your phone at home.

▷ Work up the courage to leave your phone at home when

you're going out for a walk or even out to dinner with friends. At the very least, leave the phone in your bag or your pocket on silent and resist the urge to look at it. Be brave!

SLOW READS ....

- *Unfriending My Ex: And Other Things I'll Never Do* by Kim Stolz

- *The Circle* by Dave Eggers

- *Deep Work: Rules for Focused Success in a Distracted World* by Cal Newport

EIGHT

Energy

'I just don't have enough *time*.'

How many times have you fought a losing battle with time? Time quite often seems to have the upper hand. It waits for no one and there just never seems to be enough of it.

In her book *On Time: Finding Your Pace in a World Addicted To Fast,* the journalist Catherine Blyth takes a deep dive into time to reveal why time has seemingly sped up. How is that, as our life expectancies increase and we have more time than ever, we feel so time poor? She argues that it is because our world has become addicted to fast and that we have become servants to time.[75]

From scheduling meetings to desperately scratching things off seemingly bottomless To Do lists to attempting to fit in some sort of a semblance of a personal life around work, time, or the lack of it, can feel like the enemy. Time management can feel exhausting. It can also make us feel like we're constantly failing. If our To Do lists never get fully crossed off, have we achieved our goals?

What if you focused on managing your *energy* instead of focusing solely on managing your *time*? What if we could figure out what times of day we did our best creative work, and what section of the week was better suited to admin work? What if we proved to ourselves that if we spent time exercising, that meant our energy levels made us more productive? Imagine if you made small changes to your diet and found that it helped you feel better and more productive when you were at work? Would having more energy at work help with your overall time management?

This is the core idea of the Energy Project, founded by the journalist, author and speaker Tony Schwartz. The aim of this company is to study work performance and help its clients tackle the issue of employee disengagement. Schwartz and his team pinpointed burnout as a leading cause of disengagement, and so they focused on helping individual employees avoid it by managing their energy and not their time.

'The way most of us work isn't working,' Schwartz wrote in a *Harvard Business Review* article entitled 'The Productivity Paradox: How Sony Pictures Gets More Out of People by Demanding Less'. 'Once people understand how their supply of available energy is influenced by the choices they make, they can learn new strategies that increase the fuel in their tanks and boost their productivity.'[76]

The key idea behind the Energy Project is that humans require 'four sources of energy to operate at their best: physical, emotional, mental and spiritual'. In this chapter, we're going to home in on that first leg of the chair – our physical energy.

So, how can we manage our physical energy? Let's take a look at where our energy comes in from, namely through the food we eat, how well we sleep and how often we exercise.

EAT: SLOW FOOD

Ballymaloe House in Shanagarry in Co Cork is considered hallowed ground for food folks in Ireland and around the world. Since Myrtle Allen won a Michelin star for her cooking in Ballymaloe House in the 1960s, it's been on the international food map as a beacon of great, wholesome food.

Darina Allen, Myrtle's daughter-in-law, is known for her energy at work. She opened the Ballymaloe Cookery School in 1983 and is a pioneer of the Irish Slow Food movement. Pretty much any time I've seen her in person at Ballymaloe, if she hasn't been deeply absorbed in a talk or a demonstration someone is giving, she's been on the way somewhere else, moving on to the next job that needs to be done.

I caught Darina over the phone to ask her about energy. She had a few minutes between teaching a class on her world-renowned 12-week cookery course and a sustainable food course that the school has recently launched. Our conversation is peppered with polite interruptions, such as when Darina stops someone walking past her to say, 'Will you take those brown bread loaves out of the oven now? Thank you.'

How does someone like Darina Allen manage her energy? 'I laughed when your interview request came in. If I told people around me that I thought I had a brilliant work–life balance, they'd fall about laughing, despite my good intentions. But I'm 68 and I do seem to have a lot of energy. And I think that's down to the food we eat here. Not everything I eat is organic but it mostly is. I'm very fortunate to live where I do and that very often when we sit down to meals here, almost everything on the plate has been grown by us.'

We don't all live in such food-rich environments but we could apply the tenets of slow food to at least a portion of our shopping and eating habits. There's a myth that shopping organically or locally can't be done on a budget. True, it's hard to compete with the slashed prices of enormous budget supermarkets but there's a false economy to shopping that way, as was discussed in the Money chapter.

'It's very busy here,' says Darina. 'But you know what? I absolutely love it. It doesn't even feel like work.'

Food as fuel

I used to think the idea of food as fuel was deplorable. Food isn't fuel. It's pleasure. It's joy. It's life! I thought people who viewed food purely as fuel were zero craic. But guess what? It turns out food can be both a pleasure *and* a fuel. What we put into our bodies has a direct impact on our performance and our work.

'For those of us battling to stay on top of emails, meetings, and deadlines, food is simply fuel. But as it turns out, this analogy is misleading,' writes Ron Friedman in a *Harvard Business Review* article called 'What You Eat Affects Your Productivity'.[76] 'The foods we eat affect us more than we realise. With fuel, you can reliably expect the same performance from your car no matter what brand of unleaded you put in your tank. Food is different. Imagine a world where filling up at Mobil meant avoiding all traffic and using BP meant driving no faster than 20 miles an hour. Would you be so cavalier about where you purchased your gas?'

Friedman goes on to outline how most of what we eat is transformed into glucose by our body, which helps the brain stay alert. Our attention wanes when we're low on glucose. 'So far, so obvious,' writes Friedman. 'Now here's the part we rarely consider: Not all foods are processed by our bodies at the same rate.'

Elsa Jones is a qualified nutritional therapist and author of the bestseller *Goodbye Sugar*. She works with people to redesign their diets to help manage their energy, moods, focus and weight. I ask her about how food impacts our energy and focus. She's not a fan of the short-lived energy of the sugar rush that comes from snacking on chocolate, sweets, soft drinks and biscuits. 'Unfortunately, for every up there is a down, hence the subsequent sugar crash causing our energy levels to plummet, triggering further sweet cravings.'

It's not just sugar that creates these short bursts of unsustained energy. Jones notes that 'fast-release carbohydrates like white bread and white pasta have a similar effect in that the body converts them into glucose very quickly.

The problem with regularly over-consuming these types of foods is that it can cause our blood sugar levels to go up and down like a seesaw, which has three major effects. Firstly, it wreaks havoc on our energy levels. Secondly, it causes consistent cravings for sweet and starchy foods. And thirdly, it raises insulin levels, thus encouraging our bodies to go into "fat storing mode", particularly around our mid-section.'

Jones also says that our day-to-day mental and emotional wellbeing can be impacted by excessive sugar consumption. 'If our blood sugar levels are unbalanced, it can leave you trapped in a vicious cycle of sugar highs and sugar lows when can leave you feeling tired, irritable, moody and constantly craving sugar.'

Through her personal and professional experience, she has found a low glycaemic diet to be the most effective in keeping blood sugar and insulin levels stable. Jones recommends we limit fast-release carbohydrates, include a portion of protein with every meal, get the balance between protein, slow-release carbs and vegetables right at meal times, avoid long gaps between meals by having healthy snacks like nuts, fruit, hummus and yogurt on standby, and limit stimulants. Jones recommends no more than two caffeinated drinks per day.

I feel it in my gut

If you're in any way into food, you'll be all over kombucha, kefir and kimchi. These cultured food and drinks are as old as the hills but their relevance has been gaining ground in the last five to 10 years. A resurgence in popularity among chefs, cooks and food lovers has brought these foods into the limelight, together with scientific research which can back up the benefits of the age-old method of preservation.

In other parts of Europe and around the world, the method of production that centres around fermentation has never fallen out of fashion. Back in 1985, Gaby and Hans Wieland moved to Ireland from Germany. Gaby was a nurse and Hans was a teacher, and they were looking to gain more control over the pace of their lives. After travelling around Europe looking for like-minded communities, they decided to move to a mobile home in Sligo. 'Sometimes in life,' Hans tells me, 'if you're looking for adventure, you have to take a leap of faith and go.'

The mobile home had no running water or electricity. Luckily, Hans and Gaby were already well versed in the ways of pickling, fermenting and preserving food, because of the traditional food culture of Germany. 'If you're wealthy or have a certain income you can buy your own food. If you have less income or no income, to be self-sufficient, you have to produce your own food.'

Hans grew up in a small village in Germany called Untersteinach where fermented foods were part of the fabric of food production in the community. 'The most important part of fermented foods in that village was preserving,' explains Hans. 'You wanted to make milk last longer so you made it into quark cheese. Flour doesn't last for ever so you make it into a sourdough starter, and you turned cabbage into sauerkraut.' Hans would help his grandmother in her shop by filling bags with sauerkraut from huge jars in her basement to sell to customers. Gaby is from the outskirts of Frankfurt and she remembers eating bags of sauerkraut on her way to school as a snack.

Because they spent their first two years in Ireland living in a mobile home with no water or electricity, knowing how to make sourdough bread, cheese and sauerkraut helped them survive and thrive. They eventually moved out of their mobile home but stayed in Sligo and went on to make goat's cheese under the name Cliffoney Organic Farmhouse Cheeses. They're both involved in the Organic Centre in Rossinver in Co Leitrim, where they lecture about food to this day. They are considered by many to be the foremost experts in fermentation in Ireland and they were among the key organisers of Ireland's first Fermentation Festival in 2016.

'The health benefit of fermentation is in the pre-digestion,' explains Hans. 'The food has been broken down already. Soya beans are a good example. You can't really digest them but if they're fermented and made into miso, then through the fermentation process the body can digest it and take the nutrients in. Sauerkraut actually enhances the nutrition of cabbage. Fermentation not only makes it last longer and more digestible, but it makes it nutritionally better. A lot of fermented foods are low in calories as well.

'In my own experience,' he goes on to say, 'fermented food creates a healthy gut. In turn, the healthy gut leads to a good immune system. On a personal level, I never get coughs and colds. I'm fairly healthy when it comes to the normal bugs you get in the winter or summer.'

Back at the APC Microbiome Institute in University College Cork, Dr John Cryan and his colleagues have been studying the science behind this ancient food process. You aren't just what you eat, he says, but you are what your microbes (i.e. the good bacteria that cause fermentation) eat. In a Ted Talk from July 2017, he says that 'over the last two decades, we have begun to really understand that there is a very important relationship between our microbes and our overall physiology'.[78]

Dr Cryan gives me a beginner's lesson on the science behind our microbiome (the ecosystem of microorganisms living in our gut), and the connection between our diet, our microbiome and our brain function. 'How we eat really affects our microbiome so much,' he says. 'We know, for example, that Omega 3 fatty acids, polyphenols affect the microbiome in a positive way'. Cryan explains that perhaps the positive effects that have been reported in connection to certain types of food, such as increased energy, are actually linked to their positive impact on the microbiome.

'Fermented foods like kefir, kimchi and sauerkraut are really great foods for bolstering our microbiome which in turn can positively change our brain function.' There are ongoing studies about how fermented foods can dampen down our stress response, Cryan tells me. 'People have to go to work and it's inevitable that they will get stressed, but it's how you react to that stress that counts.'

I see fermented foods as the ultimate in slow food. It's not difficult but I have killed many a kefir grain and sourdough starter through a lack of respect for its rhythm. It requires some attention and a certain modicum of routine. My friend Helen Heanue from Inishturk Island gifted me with kefir grains in the summer of 2016. It was such an honour to take these precious little microbe-rich grains back to the mainland with me to look after. It took me all of three weeks to kill them, through sheer neglect. I got too 'busy'. My life was so fractured and disorganised and frantic that I wasn't able to look after myself, let alone these kefir grains.

I tried again in the summer of 2017, towards the end of my year of working slowly. Helen gifted me with more kefir grains and this time I was determined to look after them properly. I found it easier to get into the rhythm of looking after these little live cultures. The process involves placing the grains in a jar and adding a few cups of really good-quality milk (organic and raw in my case), and then letting them sit in a warm place for 12 to 24 hours. The next step is to remove the grains from the kefir milk and store them in another jar, topped up with some good-quality milk. Then the kefir milk, which can be as thick and sour as a yogurt, is ready to be enjoyed.

That sounds easy, doesn't it? And it *is* easy, but it requires routine and a measured pace. If you're flying all over the gaff like a headless chicken going from one task to the next, it's also very *easy* to leave the kefir out on the windowsill for too long or forget about it in the fridge for a few weeks.

Well, I'm happy to report that, at the time of writing, Helen's kefir grains are alive and well. I even have a friend lined up to look after them while I go away on holidays. The process of looking after these mysterious little cultured grains that I don't fully understand, which in turn seem to be looking after me, has been a rewarding one. And I can finally show my face in Helen's Inishturk kitchen without feeling guilty about being a kefir grain murderer.

'If you look at fermentation,' Hans tells me, 'it creates really, really good food but it needs time. You can't do sourdough in an hour or two. We recently timed our own sourdough process at home, and from the start of the process to being able to eat it took 30 hours. But what you get from those 30 hours is a really, really delicious and nutritious bread which lasts two or three weeks. But it needs time to develop in the first place. Often slowing down in food production makes a much better product. If you compare that to how people work, if we slow down and focus the end product of our work will be much better than this fast-paced lifestyle. Slowing down is the future.'

Amen to that.

Coffee – sweet, sweet coffee

On a good day, my morning routine goes a little like this:

- ▷ Alarm goes off.
- ▷ Snooze gets pressed.

▷ Alarm goes off again.

▷ Get up.

▷ Head bleary-eyed to the coffee grinder.

▷ Make a cup of coffee with my trusty Aeropress.

▷ Make up a yogurt and granola cup.

▷ Practise meditating for five minutes (for me this means practising how to bring my focus back to my breathing).

▷ Sit at my desk and start the work day with a sip of coffee and a spoonful of granola.

▷ Get showered and dressed and take my first break of the day – a walk with Daffodil.

Coffee is one of my favourite parts of the day. In the evening, I look forward to tomorrow morning's coffee. I love the smell, the flavour and the power of coffee, all of which help give me a kick-start in the morning.

I go through periods of coffee abuse. I often wake up before 7 am to catch the quiet writing hours of dawn. Before my year of slow, I would regularly have had three cups of coffee on an empty stomach before 10 am. By noon I would be a manic pixie monster, hyped up on coffee, headed for an anxiety-fuelled crash.

Foods that can boost dopamine and serotonin levels – like coffee – have been found to improve people's moods.

Dopamine is a hormone involved in the reward or pleasure centre of the brain. In a 2002 study, researchers concluded that caffeine stimulates an increase in dopamine levels.[79] The old adage of everything in moderation is still at play, even with dopamine-inducing stimulants such as caffeine, which is also a psychoactive drug.

A study at La Trobe University's School of Psychological Sciences in Melbourne, Australia, found that five or more coffees a day was enough to increase the participant's tendency to hallucinate.[80] In the study, led by Professor Simon Crowe, participants with varying stress and caffeine conditions were asked to listen to white noise and report each time they heard Bing Crosby's rendition of *White Christmas* during the white noise.

People high on caffeine were more likely to hear the song. But, guess what? The classic Christmas tune was *never played* during the experiment.

Mind. Blown.

Researchers concluded that the combination of caffeine and stress affects the likelihood of an individual experiencing psychosis-like symptoms. That little experiment made me view my coffee consumption a little differently.

Elsa Jones has ideas about caffeine, too. 'Sugar along with caffeine can have a stimulatory effect on our nervous system and adrenal glands. A diet high in stimulants can increase production of stress hormones like adrenalin and cortisol which can make us feel wired, moody and anxious as well as affecting our sleep cycle.'

It's well established that there *is* such a thing as too much of a good thing. Anyone who's awoken from a night out on the town, fully dressed and using a half-eaten kebab as a pillow knows that. Better to limit what you love, within reason, than to over-indulge to a point of loathing. How long can you sustain coffee-induced mania before starting to distrust the source? For me, two cups of coffee a day works, sometimes supplemented with a cup of tea. For you, it might be one or three or none.

SLEEP

I have a shaky history with sleep. I'm a chronic sleep-talker, have regular nightmares and a penchant for sleepwalking. Once, shortly after we first met, I sleepwalked into Niall's parents' bed. Unfortunately, his dad was *in* the bed at the time. It was literally the most mortifying moment of my life.

That mortification, but also the fatigue brought on by my midnight adventures – not to mention the constant disturbance to Niall's (and his dad's) sleep – propelled me to make some lifestyle changes. My break from alcohol helped quell my night-time terrors, as did keeping a relatively tidy bedroom. Changing the position of my bed so it was facing the window also seemed to help. Why did those changes work for me? I sought out a sleep expert to find out more about how sleep impacts our work.

When I meet Deirdre McSwiney, a sleep technician and cognitive behavioural therapist for insomnia sufferers, she asks me what I'm drinking.

'A peppermint tea,' I reply, with a touch of smugness.

'Goodie-two-shoes,' she jokes.

Deirdre McSwiney has over 20 years' experience working in sleep medicine. One of her specialities is treating insomnia through cognitive behavioural therapy. 'Caffeine is not the devil,' she says in reference to my purposeful peppermint tea. 'It's very nice! And when it hits you at the right time of the day, it's very useful. But it's also a stimulant and it will keep you awake if you drink it too close to bedtime.'

McSwiney talks me through the key consequences of continuous poor sleep, namely chronic tiredness, weight gain, mood changes, frustration, difficulty controlling emotions and coping with stress, absenteeism and, according to research, an increased risk of diabetes, heart disease and some cancers.

We talk through sleep hygiene, which includes considering environmental and lifestyle factors that can inhibit a good night's sleep. Environment means light and noise, while lifestyle pertains to diet and exercise. She recommends a wind-down to bedtime that lasts two hours, with a blanket ban on phones, tablets, Kindles and laptops within that time. Exercise is essential for a good night's sleep, but it shouldn't be done within two hours of bedtime, she says. Think you're relaxing yourself with a late-night bath? McSwiney begs to differ. 'You're sending your body very mixed messages by having a bath late at night.' Sleep should be our priority. McSwiney emphasises the importance of quality over quantity.

'The most important thing,' she stresses, 'is a regular routine. That means going to bed at the same time every night. And people don't like to hear this, but it means getting up at the same time every morning, even on the weekends.'

My friend Áine works at a leading global tech company. She travels a lot for work, to meet with her teams in the US and

Asia. 'There are quite a few of us who regularly see each other on our commutes. You'll see the same faces in Dublin Airport and we're all trying to carve out time to rest so that we can arrive ready to go,' she says. Like the commuters you see every day on the train or walking the same route in the morning, there are transatlantic commuters regularly hopping on planes to make a meeting in a different time zone. What are the tricks for workers travelling through time zones – or shift workers? McSwiney recommends trying to find routine on the go. If you often stay in the same hotel while on business trips, try to get the same room each time.

And by the way, guess what else McSwiney told me? It's a myth that eating cheese late at night gives us nightmares. It's the best news I've heard all year.

EXERCISE

I'm treading water in Dublin Bay, taking in the city's coastline from a water-based vantage point at Seapoint, a popular swimming spot not too far from Dublin's city centre. To my left are the iconic Poolbeg Towers. A bruiser of a cloud is hovering over the peninsula of Howth while magic shards of light pierce through the clouds and bounce off the water. The water is chillingly cold, even in the height of our mild Irish summer, but

I'm wearing a thick wetsuit. It's so thick it even buoys me up in the water, helping me to float and take in the awesome views. I am sea swimming in the city.

Research has linked exercise to stress relief, and research continuously shows that exercise can boost our energy levels. Researchers at the University of Georgia have found that even a single bout of exercise lasting longer than 20 minutes increases our energy.[81]

You know exercise is good for you. I know exercise is good for me. But, *damn*, it can be hard to make time for it or to find the energy for it.

There are two interesting approaches that have helped me to look at exercising differently, and to ensure that it fits into my schedule. One is Stephen Guise's, explained in his book *Mini Habits: Smaller Habits, Bigger Results* and his guide to imperfectionism, *How To Be An Imperfectionist: The New Way to Self-Acceptance, Fearless Living, and Freedom from Perfectionism*. When a perfectionist sets out to do 100 sit-ups, if she does 99 she feels like a failure. So why not set out to do 10 sit-ups? And then the next day you could try 20 sit-ups. And then the next day 30, and so on, until you reach your initial target of 100. Or maybe you would stay at 30 sit-ups. That's better than nothing.

I took this same approach to the swimming pool. I decided that 10 sit-ups (or 10 laps in the pool) was better than aiming for 100. Rather than trying to get a 40-minute swim in, if I went to the pool for a short burst of 20 minutes in the water, I could be back at my desk within an hour. That was manageable and sustainable. This taps into the power of habit.

In the international bestseller *The Power Of Habit: Why We Do What We Do in Life and Business*, author Charles Duhigg explains his belief that any habit can be formed through time and effort. He sees exercise as an important milestone in overall lifestyle change. 'Typically, people who exercise start eating better and becoming more productive at work. They smoke less and show more patience with colleagues and family. They use their credit cards less frequently and say they feel less stressed. Exercise is a keystone habit that triggers widespread change.'[82]

Apart from creating the right conditions to make exercise a regular habit instead of a huge commitment of my time and a chore, the other approach I took was to find something kind of *epic*. Something that gave me a more intense hit of endorphins than a walk with my dog. And I found what I was looking for in sea swimming.

In Ruth Fitzmaurice's beautiful memoir *I Found My Tribe*, she describes how she became a converted sea swimmer as a way to cope with her husband Simon's motor neuron disease. In an interview with Roisín Ingle of *The Irish Times*, Ruth shared how one of her 'tribespeople' – her fellow sea-swimmers – described the experience of jumping into the cold Irish sea: 'You may not always like the person who goes into the water but you always like the person who comes back out.'[83]

My friend Duggy is a sea swimmer. He's also a technical lead at a multinational computer software company. He travels a lot for work but whenever he can he swims in the sea. He'll swim for hours at a time, swimming out on his own into bays unknown with a buoy tied around his ankle.

I ask him about what sea swimming does for him. 'The ocean feels like home,' he tells me. 'If I go more than a week without getting in the sea I start to feel it. I've got a bad back as well with a trapped nerve and it's the only time I get to be pain free. What started out as a way to keep fit for surfing turned into so much more.'

And what does he get from taking off into the ocean, with a mini buoy tied to his ankle for flotation? 'While unemployed it staved off depression and connected me with a community of like-minded individuals that look out for each other. It's just a treat to be able to jump in. And it doesn't matter if it's for two minutes or three hours. The feeling is the same. My day job is pretty brutal. Like drinking fire on top of a volcano. It's really reactive with constant pressure. The sea is the chance to turn off and reset between travels. It absolutely affects how I can deal with the day job. If I was religious I would say it's like getting a hug from God.'

Sea swimming has become my epic exercise. Even with my wetsuit, the cold of the ocean brings me right into the present moment. I don't have the capacity to worry about work or rent or projects or perfectionism. I'm battling with the ocean. The sea constantly changes and I need to focus on it to swim through it safely. I don't know what challenge it will bring next. I *crave* my sea swims now, as I once craved booze, because it so completely takes me out of my brain and wipes my stressy head clean.

Is there a form of epic exercise calling you? Jump in and maybe you'll find it helps you get out of that busy brain of yours.

MANAGING YOUR OWN ENERGY

So we've reminded ourselves about where we get energy *from*, but how do we learn how to *use* it wisely? How can we learn to more intentionally manage the output of our energy?

Energy awareness

Managing your own energy is about getting to know your own ebbs and flows. The artist Emily Robyn Archer is currently working on a project to help people visualise and map their own personal flows of energy. 'As an artist and creative,' she tells me, 'I noticed pretty early on that I had times of intense creative energy and times when I had much less motivation to create. Sometimes I would be in the studio late into the night with seemingly endless ideas and energy, other times I'd feel I had nothing to give. Instead of beating myself up about not being productive all of the time, I began to think about these "phases of creativity" in terms of energy cycles. If you look at nature, nothing grows and produces all of the time – there are steady cycles in which plants will root, flower, fruit, mature and compost themselves, and each of these phases is as important as the next to the life of the plant. I think we all need time to look in new directions, to create and expand but also time to go inwards, rest and reflect.'

Archer is currently working on an illustrated female energy cycle, in collaboration with yogini Lou Horgan, in an effort to better understand how this cycle impacts women's overall energy and wellbeing. 'Women have very clear energy cycles, roughly following one lunar month. Over the course of 28 days-ish our bodies build up energy and release it in what's known as the menstrual cycle. Many women still think of their menstrual cycle as a nuisance and a purely biological affair. But there is so much to it. Throughout this cycle we have phases of heightened creativity, empathy and even intuition.'

Archer's work revolves around the importance of getting to know yourself in order to help manage your energy in a way that works for you. 'We're all so different,' she says. 'What will energise one person might exhaust another. I think getting to know ourselves, our inner nature, while taking inspiration from outer nature is the best way to keep energy flowing in a positive way. Since I started noticing these inner and outer energy cycles I have a much greater sense of ease around my work. Perhaps surprisingly, I get more done as a result.'

Life's rhythm

Sister Pauline McGaley worked as the principal of a secondary school in Dublin for years before she became the director of the Warrenmount Centre in Dublin 8. I met her when I was volunteering at the Warrenmount Centre's free conversation classes for migrants living in the city. McGaley is a Presentation sister, a religious institute of Catholic women founded in Cork in the late 1700s, whose key mission is about the education of others, particularly young women. She is someone who clearly thrives on being busy, though she is starting to slow down as she reaches retirement age. She's interested in mindfulness, which the centre offers classes in, and a future goal of hers is to set up an inter-religious meditation group.

After a busy conversation class, we spoke about how she has managed her energy throughout her working and spiritual life. 'As religious women teaching in schools, we always brought our work home with us. Our reason for being a congregation was educationalist, that was our conviction and our commitment. We would spend our summers doing work on the school. Our work ethic was 120%. In terms of work–life balance, I suppose we weren't very good at it. Even at recreational times, we had the knitting out. Over the last couple of years, I have relaxed around things. That wouldn't have come naturally to me but I've been able to change. One can be more present with people when you slow down. You can miss important moments just by not paying attention. I have more time now to pay attention to people.'

Like Archer, Sister McGaley understands that this process of slowing down or finding a rhythm that works for you can be greatly helped by self-awareness. 'I think for women in religious life there is a definite rhythm to our day and life that somehow facilitates a balanced pace – prayer, work and relaxation. The success of that rhythm is dependent on personality and knowing yourself.'

Though I'm not religious, I find it interesting to think about that rhythm of prayer, work and relaxation. It's such a clear energy roadmap. For those of us who don't pray, what have we filled that slot with? More work? Is there something we can learn from this traditional model of energy management?

Where should you direct your energy?

Clare Mulvany has previously been a photographer, yoga teacher, writer, blogger, life coach. While doing this, she was running social projects and co-running Trailblaze, an Irish-based 'Ted Talks with soul' (you may remember her from the Gut chapter). 'Somehow I had the energy for it. At that time I was able to juggle it,' she tells me over coffee in The Fumbally Café. 'Recently I have noticed a shift in my needs as I get older. Rather than scattering many things in many directions, I've realised that there are some seeds that need more attention. So instead of having a forest of seedlings I would like a woodland of really solid trees. Maybe there are only a few solid trees but they are giving a lot more protection and shelter, and the roots of those trees are enriching lots of other saplings.'

Seriously, that is actually how Mulvany talks. She's like an oracle of wisdom, full of descriptive language around gut, flow and creativity.

Being able to direct your energy towards the right projects for you involves that link between your gut and your decisions. Should I use my energy to bake two dozen cupcakes in the early hours before work for the people in my office in a thinly veiled effort to get them to like me, or should I save that energy for myself so that I can be a calm, rested person to work alongside? Should I say yes to the project that will bring me great financial reward but will put me in a position of working with people who leave me feeling depleted? If your gut can be allowed a seat at the negotiating table when decisions are made, to argue it out with your heart and your mind, the decision may result in the best use of your energy.

Lizzie Fitzpatrick is the singer and lead guitarist in the explosively raucous Dublin band Bitch Falcon. The trio bring their loud and raw swagger to festivals around the country, slaying eardrums and souls with their high-energy show. By day, Fitzpatrick works as a surgical nurse in a private clinic where she has a 9 to 5, Monday to Friday role, leaving her evenings and weekends free for practising and touring with the band.

I ask her what it's like to balance what are essentially two jobs. 'I worked for a while as a nurse on a ward,' she tells me, 'and though I loved the challenge and the pace of it, I realised that I wasn't going to be able to do ward work and keep up with my music at the same time. I chose to do this type of nursing so that I could focus on music as well. If I wasn't a musician, I would like to work in the Intensive Care Unit, but I think if you want to be that kind of nurse it requires complete dedication so you just can't do anything outside of it.'

What's interesting to me about Fitzpatrick's story is how she has positioned herself in a day job that doesn't soak up all her energy. Of course she works hard as a nurse and it's tiring, like any job, but the nature of the type of nursing role she has gone into means that there is space in her brain and energy levels in her battery so that she can pursue music as well.

FINDING BALANCE IN THAT MAGIC FLOW

Most of us can relate to the notion of 'flow' at work. This is when you are *in the zone*. Your ideas are just amazing and the work is flowing out of you. You're basically a genius! Procrastinators like myself love this state, when you can *finally* get some work done. Good work, too.

'The idea in positive psychology of flow,' explains Leisha McGrath, the organisational psychologist we met in previous chapters, 'is a different set of circumstances that are individual for everybody. You're completely in the moment, you're on fire. It's exciting and there's a lot of adrenalin. But how do you disengage and come down from that? It all goes back to balance. If I go up, I must go down.'

Just like most things in life, we don't really fully understand them until we are *in* them. Like, up to our eyeballs in them (think of childbirth, losing a loved one or experiencing burnout). Often we are so programmed to achieve, and to keep going, that we have to hit the lowest of lows before we finally stop and listen – to our body, our gut, our heart. It might take being utterly crushed before we finally slow down and become still, and get to think about the life we *really* want to be living. The Energy Project calls this 'forced recovery' – a time when your body shuts down and literally forces you to recover, because you've simply been giving too much of yourself, and not intentionally renewing and restoring your energy.

This brings us back to recovery and burnout. The flow can easily tip over to creative mania, where you forget to eat, sleep and exercise – all the things we have established are essential to our performance-enhancing energy banks.

EAT, SLEEP AND EXERCISE

If you're expecting your body to be able to keep up with at least some of the pressures that you or others are putting on it, try to give your body a fighting chance by feeding it well, exercising it regularly and giving it a good night's sleep.

If that sounds frustratingly simple, I'm afraid it is simply the truth. But what's great about simplicity is that it is attainable. Believe me, I know how hard it can feel to make time for 20 minutes of exercise, or eat breakfast, or impose an email cut-off point in the evening. But once you start introducing these elements, in small steps, you soon won't be able to live without them. By prioritising these elements, you're prioritising yourself and, in turn, you're prioritising your work performance.

FIVE SLOW NOTES TO SELF ....

1. Manage your energy as well as your time.

▷ Make an investment in your energy by having a healthy approach to eating, sleeping and exercising. Figuring out your natural energy cycles (whether you're better at working on creative projects in the morning, for example) might help you manage your time better.

2. Eat.

▷ Pay close attention to what you eat. What gives you energy, real long-lasting energy? What takes it away from you?

3. Sleep.

▷ Try to keep a regular routine for bedtimes and wake-up calls. And stop looking at your phone last thing at night and first thing in the morning! It's bad sleep hygiene and there is no reason for you to do it. If you need your phone as an alarm clock, put it on airplane mode or disconnect it from the internet when it's in your bedroom.

4. Exercise.

▷ Find a type of exercise that you love and that fits into your packed schedule. Remember that even 15 minutes of exercise a day is so much better than no exercise at all. Letting go of the notion that going to the gym has to mean an investment in time of at least 45 minutes might break down the time barrier that's stopping you exercising regularly.

5. Start with small steps and mini-habits.

▷ Start with small steps, gradually introducing your body and your schedule to a healthier diet and regular exercise which should help towards getting a better night's sleep.

SLOW READS ....

- *The Way We're Working Isn't Working: The Four Forgotten Needs That Energize Great Performance* by Tony Schwartz, Jean Gomes and Catherine McCarthy

- *The Art of Fermentation: An In-Depth Exploration of Essential Concepts and Processes from around the World* by Sandor Katz

- *The Power Of Habit: Why We Do What We Do in Life and Business* by Charles Duhigg

NINE

Environment

Inishturk is an island off the coast of Co Mayo in the west of
Ireland. It's home to around 58 people and has one primary
school, one shop, one pub and one church. Its one road
is a perfect 5 km loop. On a clear day, a walk around the
island can see you enveloped in the breathtaking views of
the Connemara coastline and Inishbofin Island of Co Galway,
Croagh Patrick and Achill Island in Mayo.

Over the last three years, I've been involved in Turkfest, a
gathering of friends and friends of friends for an August
weekend of exploration and craic on the island. It's a non-
profit crowd-funded festival, sort of a large party of pals, that
happens *with* the island as opposed to *on* the island. This
party is the brainchild of my brilliant friend Fionn, whose family
have been visiting Inishturk since he was a little kid. It's a party
he's thrown since 2013, and its attendees have grown from
25 pals to a maximum capacity of 150 revellers. We organise

music in the Community Club, crab claws on the beach, a GAA football match against the islanders on what has to be Ireland's most beautiful football pitch, workshops with the islanders, a hilarious road-bowling tournament, and a heap of creamy pints of Guinness.

As the informal weekend away grew organically into an official non-profit festival, Fionn brought in friends, including the talented producers and programmers Aoife Flynn, Maria Schweppe and Conor Wilson to help him grow Turkfest while still protecting its innocent core. I was the Programme Curator and Community Manager of Turkfest in 2016 and 2017.

Before I went to Inishturk, I had a romantic notion of this island being a beacon of slow living on the outskirts of Ireland, away from the buzzing mainland. And in some ways it is. The one shop on the island is well stocked with the bare essentials of milk, tinned foods, bread and crisps, but if you forget to pack your artisanally cured Gubbeen chorizo or a jar of Katie Sanderson's Peanut Rayu sauce, you'll have to wait until your next trip to the mainland to get it. You have no choice but to be patient until someone comes to the island or you leave and come back again. Staying there for more than a couple of days forces you to be more considered about your consumer habits, particularly around food.

The internet and phone signals are strong and reliable in places but there are some areas of the island where you simply can't refresh your Instagram feed, giving it a feeling of being accessible yet removed. It's also an awesomely beautiful place, in the traditional sense of the word 'awesome', meaning you're more inclined to look up and out at the scenery rather than down and into your phone.

But life on Inishturk for the people who live there is far from slow. In fact, many of the people there are as busy as the busiest people I've come across. There are a few government subsidies in place that go some way towards supporting the resilient community, such as the twice-daily ferry to Roonagh Pier in Mayo, which has a fare for islanders and a higher fare for visitors like me. Multi-jobbing is not uncommon and often a necessity in making living there sustainable. The residents are extremely resourceful and they are *busy*. But there's an understanding that busyness is seasonal; they can get through a hectic summer when a very quiet winter lies ahead, with plenty of time for personal pursuits like crafts and walks on the island's stunning beaches.

Mary Catherine is one of those busy islanders. She's the embodiment of the old saying, 'If you want something done, ask a busy person to do it.' She was a volunteer on the Island Committee for 13 years before she became the official Community Development Coordinator, a job she undertook for over a decade. She 'retired' last year but she is still busy with running a B&B from her family home, Ocean View House. She's a great baker, famed for her apple tarts and her light, buttery scones.

Mary Catherine is doing her best to make more time for herself these days. She has the support of her daughters, who she can depend on to look after the B&B. Their support has given her the power to say no. 'There's more awareness around our own health these days,' she tells me. 'The whole world is at that, mental health awareness, and Inishturk isn't behind in that sense. Inishturk can be as busy as you want it to be.'

Exchange the word 'Inishturk' with the word 'life' and you have a saying that most of us can relate to.

My trips to this idyllic island revolved around curating a mini-festival, which required finding accommodation for 80 people and building a campsite for another 70 while figuring out how to get a band's equipment safely to the island on the ferry, how to feed 150 people from a kitchen that usually serves 20 on a busy night, and how to create a peak craic environment while keeping everyone safe. It involved creating a paid island intern programme to involve some of the younger islanders in our production process, and dealing with the challenges that the epic weather changes on the island threw at us. So my time spent on the island wasn't exactly an exemplification of slow. I had made Inishturk a busy place for me, too.

On my island trips leading up to Turkfest 2017, I was also working on this book. I would get up early in the morning at Fionn's family's holiday home and set myself up at their writing desk, conveniently located by a window that looked out towards the glacial mountain range of Killary Harbour and the uninhabited island of Inishdalla. In the spring, baby lambs would literally walk right past the window, looking for their mammies, with an epic backdrop of their home, this island in the sea.

These were quiet, peaceful and very productive writing sessions. But I have a feeling they were so productive because they were paired with morning swims in the sea and lungfuls of fresh ocean air. Would that productivity have prevailed if I had stayed on the island, isolated, in the long term? Or would my fear of failure follow me to my island respite?

It got me thinking about environment and its impact on our pace of work. Sure, it's naive and limiting to think that if you could only just live in a cottage on an island off the west coast of Ireland, you would never feel stressed or overworked. Believe me, that is not true. However, though it may not be a fix-all cure, your environment has a significant impact on your work.

YOUR DESK

Have a look at your desk. Is it a personal organiser's dream or a cluttered cacophony of chaos? Perhaps it's somewhere in between.

Sarah Reynolds is a professional organiser. Through her website, Organised Chaos, she's been sharing tips on work, home and virtual organisation since 2012.

'Our environment impacts hugely on our productivity,' says Reynolds. 'I believe the vitality of a company is reflected in the visuals, and to me a visually deteriorating business indicates a business in decline.' This can be translated to your own desk, whether that's in a busy office or at your kitchen table.

'According to my research,' says Reynolds, 'particularly around the book *The Organized Mind* by Daniel Levitin, the brain is an energy economiser. If you have all this multiple stimuli going on in your outer environment, it's going to affect your mental environment in there. There is so much going on. If we think about all of the information that is coming towards us – we have to raise our families, clean our houses, go to work, keep up with social media, process information in emails … Our brains find it hard to cope.'

We have to set up as many external systems in our external environment as we possibly can because that reduces the burden on the brain. Whether it's a decluttered desk or how you manage your time, these are all systems in our external environment that are going to help our internal environment.

Reynolds acknowledges the idea of having a 'creative mess' of a desk, but it's her belief that your work is more focused if you have fewer distractions around you. 'If you want to increase your productivity, to get more done in a shorter space of time, then you need to reduce the amount of distractions in your environment.'

But, wait, that doesn't sound very slow …?

'The work that you're doing may not be slow,' says Reynolds. 'You may be up against a very intense deadline, but your focus on it and your approach to that work is. Because your environment is clear, you come from a different state of being than if you are trying to do all this work, up against this deadline, and then all of a sudden there's a piece of paper that you need but you can't find it, and then you remember Mary has it but you can't call her because you've just realised your phone is out of battery ... It's amazing what your third eye is able to pick up on and you just want to be able to work on exactly what is in front of you for the time that you have available to you.'

YOUR OFFICE

How can we influence environments that are out of our control? Many of us don't have control over environmental aspects like lighting and temperature, nor can we escape the noise interruptions that come with an open-plan office. There are varying degrees of limitations on how much office workers can influence and change their work environments, depending on the culture of a workplace.

Hot-desking in large, open-plan offices has become increasingly prevalent, encouraged by the advent of wireless technology. Hot-desking is where employees don't have an assigned desk. Instead, they move around, bringing their company-supplied laptop with them. It's said to decrease costs for employers by up to 30% and encourage collaboration.[84]

But is there a lack of autonomy that comes with this anti-territorial set-up? Occupational psychologist at the University of Wolverhampton Dr Jane Carstair says: 'Having your own space allows you to gain control within that small environment and personalise it with pictures and little things that define your identity. The threats to that of the non-territorial office can result in a lack of motivation and even stress.'[85]

Research has suggested that giving employees influence over their immediate office environments can lead to increased productivity. In a 2010 study, Craig Knight, director of the Identity Realization workplace consultancy, and Alex Haslam conducted a study with 47 office workers in London. Knight and Haslam argued that work spaces that don't allow their employees to have input into the design of their office environment 'may compromise organisational outcomes by disempowering workers'.[86]

They're not talking about employees being involved in drawing up architectural plans for buildings. Instead, they're talking about things like choice of artwork and the addition of plants. Through a series of experiments, their study found that workers who were allowed to self-decorate a space were up to 32% more productive. It also positively impacted on team morale and increased efficiency.

In 2014, the co-CEO of American design and architectural firm Gensler, Diane Hoskins, wrote in the *Harvard Business Review* that her firm's workplace study clearly identified choice and autonomy in the design of office space as being linked to happiness, motivation and performance, particularly in the case of knowledge workers.[87]

So there appears to be an argument for self-government in the office environment, even if that just means the ability to add a potted plant or put up a photo of your beloved pet, niece or spouse.

A LITTLE CUP OF TEA IN A FRUIT GARDEN

Remember when I was talking about Darina Allen and her seemingly endless energy? Well, we also talked about the impact of her environment on her experience at work.

'I feel very fortunate to live in the middle of a 100-acre organic farm and gardens,' she told me. 'Everywhere I look there's something beautiful. Even as I'm speaking to you now, I'm looking out the window and I can see a wonderful rose bush tumbling over what we call the *Palais du Poulet* – the hen houses. At the other side, there's a fruit garden. I can pop out there and sit on the bench and have a little cup of tea. Even ten minutes can feel like taking an hour off.'

Granted, we don't all live in Ballymaloe, and Darina is aware of that. 'Even if you work in a high-rise office block, if you can find a space that you can escape to, that could really help. If one can discipline oneself to take a five-minute break in a beautiful place, if you're fortunate enough to have access to one, that can make a huge difference to your day. If I was working in an office, I'd have a lovely big pot plant on my desk and fresh flowers in vases, and I would make my environment as lovely as possible. Here on my and my PA Sharon's desk, there's a little bundle of sweet peas. We don't even really think about gathering those flowers and putting them our desk, it's just something we do, but it's very important to us.'

THE TYRONE GUTHRIE CENTRE

'This place is like a touchstone for people's creativity,' Robbie McDonald tells me. We're talking about creative spaces over tea and scones in the old-fashioned kitchen of a country manor in Co Monaghan, nestled in the midst of dense Ulster woodland. Four hundred and fifty acres of it, to be precise. Outside, the tended gardens are in full bloom and the summer sun shimmers on Annaghmakerrig Lake. This is the Tyrone Guthrie Centre, a residential workplace for artists of all disciplines. Robbie is the centre's director.

The founder of this centre, Sir William Tyrone Guthrie, was
a renowned theatre director who left the house to the Irish
state when he died in 1971 to be used as a retreat for artists,
with one particular condition – that artists would meet for a
meal once a day. During his lifetime, Guthrie was an influential
presence in the world of theatre in the UK and the US, and
would often bring his theatre troupes, including actors such as
Alec Guinness, home with him to Annaghmakerrig to hammer
out the final details of a play. Today, artists can apply for
residencies here for a minimum of a week or a maximum of
two months, staying in one of the 11 rooms in the house or in
one of the five self-catering cottages.

'One week here is worth two at home, that's what the artists
say,' explains Robbie. 'This is a working house.' Apart from
having dinner with fellow residents every evening at 7 pm,
other rules include no pets and no partners. In the house, the
residents have their meals provided for them, and the rooms
are turned. The distractions of everyday life are minimised.
'Everything conspires to interrupt the artist. What we provide
here is time, with no interruptions, good WiFi, a photocopier
and a printer. Above all, we trust and respect the artists and
their work. We present a serene stage with an old-fashioned
welcome.'

The dinner provides an opportunity for collaboration, feedback and a sharing of work woes.

Robbie shows me through the house. The interiors evoke the early 1900s. We pass through drawing rooms and a library filled with relics of Guthrie's time here, while upstairs we poke our heads into one of the bedrooms. It's ensuite with a double bed, antique dressers and wardrobe, and a large old writing desk placed in front of the corner window with views of the lake. The only pieces of modernity are the ergonomic desk chair and the WiFi. We walk through a music room, where two composers are tinkering on the ivories of a grand piano, finishing a piece they're working on.

Outside the house, behind the painters' and printers' studios, past the rows of strawberry plants growing in formation in a small but elegant garden, lies a dance studio. Here I meet David Ferguson, a Canadian choreographer, dancer and artist. He and his partner, Miles Lowry, are the founding artistic directors of Suddenly Dance Theatre based in Victoria, British Columbia, Canada. They've been coming to Annaghmakerrig bi-annually for 25 years. 'Some artists value their time here in terms of how many words they write but for me, it's more about the state of mind I enter when I come here. Being here can open the door to my creativity. As an artist, when you've found your triggers and gateways, you have to trick yourself

271

into recreating those. Here at Annaghmakerrig, it very quickly opens people up.'

Towards the back of the house, a pretty stone building is home to the laundry room. Tess Brady, a poet from Pittsburgh, is leaving Annaghmakerrig for meetings in Dublin. 'I needed some clean socks,' she says. After a productive day of writing the previous day, she's using the morning to catch up on admin and to check in on world politics.

'We live in an age of high anxiety,' she says. 'Technology supports a constant need to be connected to something outside of ourselves, without giving space for real contact with others or even with yourself. To get to the wholeness and dream space of creativity, you need to be still. Annaghmakerrig gives you the freedom to not have to worry about the mundane or the everyday. It takes you out of the real world and provides the steadying effect of an old place. The spirit of this place remains the same.'

Towards the end of our talk, an Irish playwright stops by and asks if the washing machines are free. 'I'm procrastinating,' she admits. 'I've already washed two pairs of jeans this week.'

CHANGING YOUR ENVIRONMENT

A change is as good as a break, right? So how does changing your environment impact your ability to work? Roisín Agnew is an Irish writer whose work has featured in *The Irish Times*, *Vice* and *The Pool*, among others. She was the editor and publisher of *Guts*, a confessional writing magazine featuring words and illustrations from Irish scribes and scribblers, which both myself and my husband contributed to.

Last year, she upped sticks and left Dublin for Lisbon. Had she gone for a job? Nope. She went to find some space. 'I decided to move to Lisbon because I wanted a break from Dublin. I was finding it impossible to enjoy anything, I'd stopped really wanting to go out, I hated my job, and my achievements failed to register with me or give me any real pleasure. In hindsight I was suffering from burnout syndrome. I hadn't stopped since I was 15. I'd done my best in school, done my best in college, gone straight into a series of part-time jobs and internships, and then four different jobs back to back while maintaining a personal project and some freelance work. I never took a gap year or went travelling. My situation is unexceptional, most people live like that, but it doesn't make it any more sustainable.'

She had visited Lisbon before and found it laid-back, cheap and progressive. The weather and the southern European culture encourage a slower pace, with an emphasis on having a good quality of life rather than working as hard as possible. 'There isn't the same level of competition for who is the most overworked, most stressed, most unhappy – people seem to get a grim form of satisfaction from that in Dublin. In Lisbon people take pride in getting enjoyment out of their lives. When you get here Portuguese people feel the need to defend themselves against a stereotype that apparently portrays them as lazy. But to me it seems more that they feel no guilt about enjoying life and not wanting it to be unpleasant or stressful – why should anyone need to defend that?'

For Agnew, slowing down gave her the space she needed to tune into what she really wanted to do. She's found more time to socialise and exercise, and ultimately feels more creative because she can take more time with the things she's choosing to spend her time on. Has her experience taught her that we can slow down and still keep up?

'I think we need to abandon the idea of "keeping up" entirely. This idea about being productive has become a sort of contemporary sickness. We don't allow for the idea of *not* being productive. Culturally, being productive has become a total obsession and status symbol. My answer is you can have a better *type* of productive if you slow down, but probably not *more* productive. You can be more connected to your own desires and ambitions, understand your own skill set better, and ultimately be healthier if you slow down. Unhappy workers make for unsuccessful companies, research shows, and perhaps it's a fact that could be applied to yourself.'

Too much change?

When I get stuck creatively, particularly when I'm writing, I've found that changing my environment can be just the distraction I need to become focused. I temporarily move my office to a café for a couple of hours. The difference in noise, smells and light can be just what I need to dislodge the block. But what if your work environment was constantly changing? Would that mean that you were constantly unblocked and continuously inspired? Or would you crave a routine?

David Prior is a writer and contributing editor for publications including *Condé Nast Traveler*, *The New York Times Style Magazine* and *Vogue*. He's Australian and has a base in New York but his working life is mostly spent on the road. 'I worked out that of the last 1,222 days, 957 were on the road. So I've spent nearly 1,000 days on the road in the last three and a half years.'

I wonder how his ever-changing environment impacts on his creativity. Does it hinder or hamper it? He talks about the challenge of travel writing as having to capture the essence of a place when you have physically moved on to somewhere else. He had just come from Milan and was finishing off a piece about Milan's fashion industry while in Ireland. He shared some advice he'd been given by the food writer Kevin West: 'Do it now, to write it in the moment.' It's great advice but sometimes a writer's creativity doesn't want to play ball. 'Sometimes the creativity doesn't come,' says Prior. 'Sometimes three words will come, sometimes you'll get the whole thing.'

When he's on the move so much, what does his working environment look like? Does he get all his work done on planes, trains and automobiles? 'I can tell you I've never once done something that's creative or worthwhile while writing on the plane. Planes are not the place to write. They're good to do admin work but creativity on a plane just doesn't work for me. Trains, on the other hand, are a very creative space for me. When I was living in Italy, if I needed to write something I would get a train somewhere. It still had that white noise motion, but no WiFi. It didn't have the distractions of Instagram and email.

'A changing environment is good to be inspired and challenged, and to be a sponge. But I think when you're writing, you want the same desk and the same organised space. You want to come back to the same space. There's a lot to be said for a routine. Routine allows the thoughts to come back to you. It allows you to step back a bit from being in the moment. As a travel writer, the only routines that you can have are things that are able to be replicated. I like to run and go to the gym but you can't go for a run in the streets of Bangkok or find a gym in the Himalayan mountains.

'One of the things that has really helped me is a meditation practice two times a day for 20 minutes. That can be done on a plane. It's easy. I feel like that's one of the few things I can do in a routine. It became a total necessity because I was hurtling from place to place and dropping the ball in lots of different ways. I also try to find a gym wherever I travel. The only other thing that is really routine is coffee – it might be damaging but it's a routine!'

And how does Prior cope with the uncertainty of his industry? The established media is in a state of flux. 'Everyone is racing to a destination they don't know because the landscape has shifted so dramatically. Nothing is certain. Right now it's a moment for sprinting. It's not sustainable but everyone is sprinting. Either they're running away from what's inevitable, or they're running towards the unknown.

'I don't think people are slowing down. Everyone is reacting to SEO targets on the web, or the need to pump out three articles a week, or focusing on social media likes. It's very difficult right now with a lot of pressures to meet from different angles, both real and self-imposed. But people can't continue at this pace.

'I did a deep-dive in India for an assignment. It was a big project that I'd worked on for a long time. It was really well thought out. It wasn't a scramble. It was much more deliberate. I learned that if I can do one thing really well and really comprehensively, it will resonate with people much more. Hopefully in the future that's how I'll be able to work. I'll have time to consider my work. What is it that I want to say? What is my perspective? What is enduring or powerful? What is part of my contribution to the landscape? Those are the voices that will shine through later on.'

A different pace at home

Ard Bia is one of the most vibrant and bustling restaurants in Ireland, and it has been since it opened in Galway in 2002. Its menu is innovative and always ahead of the game in terms of trends. Not that they care about trends. They're blazing their own trail. The loveens at Ard Bia think of Galway as the centre of the universe and they like to boast about its fantastic produce on their menu. It's one of my favourite places to eat in the country, and has been for a good 15 years now.

Its owner, Aoibheann McNamara, is a personal hero of mine. She's a complete original who calls everyone 'darling'. She's endlessly generous about supporting and championing creative talent, whether it's the chefs in her kitchen, writers she admires or her friends who organise visual arts events on Irish islands. She's also one half of the Tweed Project, the slow fashion company we met in our Money chapter.

And she's high energy. Her working life at the restaurant is very busy. Her mind is busy with creative ideas with the Tweed Project. She constantly seeks out inspiration in her effort to live an aesthetic life. So when she was designing her home for herself and her son, Oni, she knew she wanted a serenely calm environment. Her home is a refurbished garage in Galway City, an open-plan living space with concrete floors, sheepskin rugs, a giant map of Iceland and Moroccan tea trays that have been turned into coffee tables. But what it doesn't have is a lot of tech. 'A few people have come to my house and have spoken about the amazing sense of peace,' says McNamara. 'There is no radio, no TV, no music and no internet in my house. My life is so busy that I wanted my home to be very peaceful.'

Her home is special and inspiring, conducive to slowness and creativity. The open-plan kitchen and living space can fit about 30 people, and McNamara often gathers folks together for a creative task, such as wreath-making, or an absorbing talk. I've been the MC for a number of talks she has hosted in the house, interviewing the food writer Trish Deseine, cooks Katie Sanderson and Jasper O'Connor, and the Buddhist monk the Venerable Panchen Ötrul Rinpoche. 'I only open it up to creative events and people wanting to pursue that.'

Every time I come home after spending time in Aoibheann's house, I get rid of a bit of clutter. The idea of minimalism applied to our domestic homes and workplaces definitely speaks to me on my quest for a slower environment – though I may not throw *everything* away just yet.

Fiona Falconer and her husband, Malcolm, left their busy lives in London to move with their children to a Wexford farm in search of the good life. They wanted to teach their kids about growing food so they planted fruit and vegetables on their land. They soon had such an abundance that Fiona and Malcolm launched a jam, chutney and syrup company called Wild About. They're now *really* busy with their growing range of delicious products. So they left busy London lives for busy Wexford lives – but there's a difference, and it's a big one.

'The real difference,' Fiona tells me, 'is that the environment we live in is incredibly therapeutic. We take a walk around our farm or pop down to the beach for a swim at teatime. We have an easier environment to engage in. We watch the seasons change, not from cancelled trains but from seeing the leaves fall. We work long hours here – no different to any small business – but we don't have that extra level of stress.'

Fiona and Malcom's story highlights the way 'busyness' can follow us anywhere, but some environments make that pace more palatable. You could thrive in a big city or maybe you yearn for teatime sea swims. If you're flexible in your work (i.e. you might simply need a laptop and an internet connection), why not experiment with the environment to see if it makes an impact on your relationship with work?

THE WELLNESS SYNDROME

Over the years, I've visited a number of corporate headquarters in the retail and tech sectors. These buildings are a veritable checklist of good architectural and design practice when it comes to their employees' wellbeing. They are flooded with natural light. There is healthy food in the canteen and unlimited tea and coffee. There are unhealthy snacks too, but they're in the bottom drawer. There are beach volleyball courts in the middle of multi-storey offices. There are gyms, nap pods and ping-pong tables.

If your company has made great and sincere efforts to make your external environment comfortable and stimulating, even if it's purely to promote productivity, it can provide a very convenient distraction to the impact its culture has on your internal environment. But if the actions of your micro-managing boss are undermining and eroding your self-confidence, having easy and unlimited access to a ping-pong table doesn't offer a long-term solution.

And if your boss is you, then the saying that 'wherever you go, there you are' needs even closer attention. Even if you moved to an island off the coast of Ireland, you'd still bring your constant roommate with you. Yourself.

In saying that, making positive changes to your environment, whether it's decluttering your office space or putting a plant pot on your desk or listening to music or creating silence, will have an influence on your productivity. Curating my own external work environment has helped me to be more productive at work while creating a calmer internal work experience.

FIVE SLOW NOTES TO SELF ....

1. Declutter.

▷ Declutter your office space as an experiment to see if you feel more focused.

2. Bring nature inside.

▷ See if a potted plant makes you feel any differently about your desk, as studies suggest.

3. Sounds and smells.

▷ Be mindful of what kind of sounds and smells are good (and not so good) for you at work. Communicate with colleagues or those who share your work space with you about what works for you in terms of noise, interruptions and smells. I think it's totally reasonable to ban tuna sandwiches in the office if they make you want to hurl.

4. Change your environment (but not too much).

▷ If you're stuck on a problem at work, a change of scene might help bring you a new perspective. Head to a café or to a different part of your office, and see if a change of scene helps get the creative ideas flowing.

5. Wherever you go, there you are.

▷ Remember that wherever you go, you bring yourself with you. Your environment has an impact on your productivity at work but it can't change who you are. Work to make the environment you have the most conducive to your working life, rather than day-dreaming about a cottage in Connemara or a minimalist office space.

SLOW READS ....

- *The Organized Mind: Thinking Straight In The Age of Information Overload* by Daniel Levitin

- *Organised* by Sarah Reynolds

- *The Best Place to Work: The Art and Science of Creating an Extraordinary Workplace* by Ron Friedman, PhD

TEN

Recovery

If you're anything like me, you'll know what it feels like to have a stressful day off. Maybe it's because your Past Self over-promised on how many cupcakes you would bake for your family gathering, not caring that your Present Self is exhausted after a huge week at work. Or maybe you're struggling with the tension of trying to enjoy being at a best friend's wedding while nipping off to the bathroom to send work emails.

Here's a potentially life-changing fact:
Recovery.
Time.
Is.
Part.
Of.
Your.
Job.

To me, respecting recovery time is perhaps the single most transformative takeaway I got from researching and writing this book.

My priorities have always been imbalanced in favour of work. If I had plans to go for a swim, it would be ignored in favour of crossing 'urgent' work items off the To Do list. My back would be in bits, screaming at me to give it attention, care and exercise, and I just wouldn't make it a priority. I would simply ignore it. If it wasn't my back that was being neglected, it was my husband or my dog. I prioritised my To Do list over proper lunch breaks, or even just a five-minute break.

These days, my swims have become a part of my working week. They aren't something I do as an extra-curricular downtime activity. Swimming, whether it's in the gym pool, the Irish Sea or the Atlantic Ocean, is a massively important part of my work week. Taking the time out to swim twice a week and look after my banjaxed back means I can be better at my work. It's non-negotiable. That goes for lunch breaks (though I don't give myself too hard a time over the odd lunch at my desk day – it happens) and mini-breaks, too.

'There are a lot of parallels between work and sport,' says Derval O'Rourke, and she would know. She is an Irish sprint hurdles athlete and the Irish national record holder for the 60 and 100 metres hurdles, who has competed at Indoor and Outdoor World Championships and three Olympics. 'It's about performance. In athletics, you train really well, you eat really well and you recover really well. If you did any of them badly, generally you wouldn't perform very well.'

O'Rourke was trained by a husband and wife team, Terrie and Sean Cahill, for eight years. At the beginning of the year, Terrie would create a plan for the following 12 months of O'Rourke's life. She would chart a flow of training, performance and recovery time, adapting the amount of recovery time to suit the extremity of the performance situation. For example, a longer recovery time would be scheduled in after a World Championships. Sometimes O'Rourke's job was to *not* work. It was to go hang out with her friends and recover.

'In sport, you take the recovery time and you would never, ever feel guilty about it. It's part of training. I think people in the corporate world feel guilty about taking recovery time, and I think people get burnt out because of that. I think it's really important for everyone who is trying to perform at a high level to factor in strategic recovery time, to avoid burnout.'

In this chapter, I'm putting forward the case for time-off activities which speak 'slow' to me. The kinds of activities that are analogue and require a different kind of focus. Ones that consume you in a restorative way so that work truly leaves your mind, and nourish you so that you can return to your desk feeling truly rested.

CRAFTS

'Crafts are a perfect expression of the Slow philosophy,' Carl Honoré wrote in his 2004 international bestseller, *In Praise of Slow*.[88] In my own quest for a slower approach to life and work over the last few years, I've found myself actively seeking out craft- and skills-based downtime activities. It all began with a pair of wedding bands.

Myself and Niall were planning our DIY wedding back in 2014, and the task we had set ourselves of creating the *best night ever* for more than a hundred of our nearest and dearest had begun to overshadow the whole point of the thing: our marriage. We were running around doing wedding jobs, ticking things off our multi-page wedding spreadsheet, as if we were curating an intimate food and music festival that our success as human beings depended on. Six months to the big day, and the next item on our To Do list was our wedding ring workshop.

At the time, the Irish Design Shop on Dublin's Drury Street (we met them in our Money chapter) offered a wedding ring workshop for couples to design and make their own rings. Over two days we sawed, soldered and shaped our individual wedding bands from rose gold. We loved the outcome, but the process was just as special. It gave us respite from the rush and anxiety that can hijack the modern wedding, by giving us a task that required slowness, focus and care.

In Ireland, we are blessed with a craft heritage which means that the opportunity to slow down by learning something new is easily attainable. Ciaran Hogan and his father Joe Hogan teach classic and artistic basket-making, either in the Spiddal Arts Village or at their home studio on the stunning Lough na Fooey in Connemara. Ciaran mostly teaches beginners from a variety of different backgrounds, usually with a shared interest in crafts or perhaps a wish to reconnect to a heritage skill like basket-making. 'You get people that would have seen their father or uncle make baskets and who always wanted to give it a go but never got around to it,' explains Ciaran.

Over a two-day workshop, Ciaran showed us how to weave wicker baskets in the traditional Connemara style. The weekend gave us time to reconnect with each other but it also helped us tap into a different way of thinking. Basket-making requires focus, and it gave us the opportunity to step away from the digital backlog and noise of our hyper-connected lives. 'People have a perception that basket-making is relaxing and therapeutic, which I think it is,' says Ciaran, 'but I also think it is challenging at parts.' He's not kidding. 'I think what people find about it is that you are so focused on the basket that it clears your mind that way, you're not thinking while making the baskets about any worries you might have in life.'

At a deeper level of immersive skills-based retreat is Lens and Larder, a food styling and photography workshop hosted by food writers, cooks and photographers Imen McDonnell (who we met alongside her husband Richard in our Burnout chapter) and Cliodhna Prendergast. They host two- to three-day workshops in beautiful Irish houses, such as Cloughjordan House in Tipperary, and invite seriously world-class photographers and food stylists to share their knowledge with small groups of food photographers, cooks, bakers and stylists.

'I think the main reason our participants relax is that we try to connect the story of the food by introducing them to the producers, the landscape where the food grows, and give them the time to put that story together in their minds and through their lens,' explains Prendergast.

'The retreats are very much steeped in nature and what surrounds us in the quiet of the countryside in most cases,'

McDonnell elaborates. 'We have often asked students to be mindful and still while sipping woodland tea made over a campfire in the quiet of the forest which I think really helped the students to relax outside of their comfort zone and really open up to more learning.'

Whether it's an afternoon of focus on a new skill, or a three-day retreat that could be a crossroads in your personal or professional life, a get-away like this can slow down your mind and help you declutter some of the buzzing thoughts that spin around your head. Organisational psychologist and life coach Leisha McGrath believes giving yourself space to create can have a powerful effect.

'We all have a natural tendency to be creative, even if we don't see ourselves being creative people,' she says. 'Creating is a really healthy and restorative thing to do, and it can take you out of the day-to-day running around while allowing you to have a gentle, nurturing space. It's about pace and focus. Taking the time to do something you enjoy is what's giving you that lasting feeling of nourishment. These types of workshops allow you to be creative, while challenging you to think in a different way, and perhaps encouraging your mind to enter a more natural state of being.'

Hogan agrees. 'A lot of people are living in cities and maybe not working with their hands, so it is a nice change to come out to Spiddal or Lough na Fooey and work with a natural material like willow. It is something very different from their normal life.'

'We are very tech-focused in life now,' says Aoibheann McNamara of Ard Bia in Galway. 'I think working with our hands, whether making bread, knitting or creating something, is very important. The time it takes, the slowness and the sense of worth one feels having created and produced something intrinsically Irish or real is a great thing.'

Of course, my fellow perfectionist over-achievers out there have to be mindful that they don't apply the same strict and unreasonable standards to their craft get-aways as they do to their regular work and life. It would be easy to let the anxiety that surrounds the quest for perfection to enter this realm of crafty downtime. 'If I don't make the best basket in this class on my first attempt,' the perfectionist might fret while weaving wicker, 'then that proves what I have always feared: I suck, at all things, for ever.'

As I've referenced in this book before, in his book *How To Be An Imperfectionist* Stephen Guise talks about the need for perfectionists to care less about the result, and more about the process. It's this great advice that I would recommend those in need of time off, but not sure how to break away from their negative thinking patterns, should keep in mind when embarking on a craft-based weekend. The point is not whether your basket is lumpy and crooked, but whether it helped you switch off from work.

GARDENING

Michael Kelly had an epiphany while buying Chinese garlic in an Irish supermarket. He didn't know it at the time but that garlic led him on a ten-year journey that saw the creation of GIY Ireland (Grow It Yourself) and the launch of a growing centre, a café and food education centre called Grow HQ on Dunmore Road in Waterford, which opened in September 2016. Kelly and his team are on a mission to educate people about the joys and benefits of growing your own food, breaking down the barriers of where food is grown, cooked and eaten. In the centre's stunning café, the menu is the product of a close collaboration between its Head Chef JB Dubois and GIY's Head Gardener Richard Mee.

'Growing food is a triple whammy of fun,' says Michael, as we sit down for a chat in the café at Grow HQ. 'When you plant it, when it starts to grow and when you eat it. But we're running a business here at the end of the day, albeit with a great mission. It's busy, busy, busy. Sometimes it's tough to stay connected to work–life balance and mindfulness.'

Kelly himself found out early on in his growing life that he could soothe his stress by going out in the garden. 'Leaving aside all the physical benefits,' he tells me, 'I think what gardening does is it gets you out of your head and into your hands. You have to by default focus on what you're doing when you're growing.'

The GIY Ireland team have transferred this experience of mindfulness in the garden through their corporate outreach programmes. They created an outdoor food garden for their clients at Diageo, where employees were broken into teams and a semi-competitive element over the gardens was encouraged. The response was phenomenal, says Kelly. The staff would go down to the garden on their lunch breaks, get out in the sun and get their hands dirty. It was a great leveller between senior and junior staff, who could work on the gardens together.

From that first corporate garden, they developed a programme that includes creating physical gardens, linking teams with local community gardens, or even something as simple as 'al desko growing', a plant you can grow in a cup and keep at your desk.

'The physical, mental and maybe even spiritual benefits of growing have a huge impact,' says Kelly. 'We've really noticed a growing emphasis on employees' wellness in the corporate sector. I'm always struck by how centred I feel after I spend time in the veg patch, and I think the same principles apply to people in the corporate sector.'

VOLUNTARY WORK

When Trump's administration tried to introduce what became known as the Muslim Ban, I felt simultaneously enraged and helpless. The only step I felt I could take to fight back at this large-scale discrimination and proliferation of the deliberately divisive, disgusting and dangerous idea of Us vs Them was to somehow get more involved in my own community.

Fáilte Isteach is a programme that welcomes migrants through conversation English classes. It's a project of Third Age, a group that specialises in connecting retirees with voluntary projects. At Fáilte Isteach, they also welcome non-retired volunteers who are able to give up their time, like myself. For a period of nine weeks, I gave up an hour and a half of my time each week to sit and talk to a couple of non-native English students. I spoke with people from Eastern Europe and the Middle East, coming from diverse backgrounds in Ireland for work, study or to be with their families.

The programme is run out of the Warrenmount Centre in Dublin 8, a community education centre founded in 1995 on the grounds of a Carmelite convent. Its founding director, Sister Pauline McGaley, whom we met in our chapter on Energy, is a Presentation sister and a former school principal. The centre's original mission was to provide education support to the local community in the area, which was at that time a designated disadvantaged area. The area has seen a huge change in the last 20 years, not just in its socio-economic make-up but in the integration of a new multinational community.

My hour and a half per week, in big picture terms, will have zero impact on world events. But it made a difference to me and, I hope, the people I spoke to at those short sessions. 'I always say that I learn more from the students than they learn from me,' jokes Alicia, one of the regular volunteers, an energetic and busy retiree. She has been volunteering at the Warrenmount Centre since she retired from her HR job in AIB in 2003. (Incidentally, Alicia says that in hindsight, the only thing she would change about her approach to work is to not worry as much.) 'I would have had pre-conceived notions about what people from different countries were like. When you meet the men and women in our classes, you hear their stories and you realise what it's like in their countries. You see the normalities of their life and what they've gone through to be here. Volunteering means you're out meeting people, and that's important, too.'

They say there's no such thing as a selfless act. While I'm not sure if that's exactly true, what's more important is that I don't think the selfish side of being 'selfless' is something we should even be ashamed of. If you're using your time off, whether it's once a year or twice a week, to support a cause that is important to you, and find it to be a nourishing mode of recovery, I would see that as a win—win.

THE CRAIC

'This is the *craic*!'

While the Danes have *hygge*, the Irish have the craic. Perhaps our heritage of story-telling, dancing, singing and enjoying the odd drop has led to many of us just being instinctively and naturally talented at having a laugh.

Sally Foran is a bona fide craic expert. She is a DJ and creative, living and working in Dublin. She is known for being a talented party starter and tune curator, and she is sort of like the long-lost sister of Frida Kahlo and the Chiquita banana lady. Her clothes reflect the bright colour and spark of her personality and talent; she wears wide flowing skirts, jangly bangles on her wrists and her own homemade headdresses assembled from flowers or pompoms.

I asked her if she could define craic. What is it? 'Craic is the sparkle you cannot see,' she says. 'The zing that makes your belly flip. The thought or memory that enters your head and makes you laugh out loud when alone on public transport. It's the the look, nod or wink from a stranger to let you know they're up for a fleeting adventurous interaction. It's the joy. It's the fuck it, why not. Craic is for the hell of it. Do it till you cry, or to make someone stop crying.'

The craic feels so quintessentially Irish that it's a surprise to read on Wikipedia that the word is actually derived from the Middle English *crak*, meaning loud conversation or bragging talk. 'Crack' as conversation or news is used in Northern England and Scotland. It may have travelled to Ireland from Scots through Ulster, as late as the mid-twentieth century, and became Gaelicised into 'craic' somewhere along the way.

So the word 'craic' was imported. But it is something that Irish people appear to have a natural, though of course not exclusive, affinity with.

But what about if work has you so burnt out that you've forgotten how to have the craic? Your internal battery is too low and you cannot access your will to have the craic?

'Not everyone is as good at craic as others,' explains Foran. 'If you're particularly good at it then you're socially responsible, I think, to make others better at it. Sometimes people don't always respond the way you'd hoped to craic because they weren't expecting it but later I'm sure they'd think of it and wish they'd guffawed or joined in like their little child inside was screaming for them to do.'

How can we recognise the craic dealers among us? 'If someone has a high level of craic you can usually see it beaming from their eyes or mouth,' Sally explains. 'Those, however, who are "craictose intolerant" will have a furrowed brow and a crooked grin. Cheesy, dopey grins are ones to look out for. We all need craic to keep us alive and sane and silly. I'm not saying craic is something you should be thinking about how to do too much, all I'm saying is if you're the kind of person who can pass a bowl of fruit and not answer the banana as if it were a telephone, then I don't think you're having enough craic.'

Some ideas for sparking craic from Sally include:

▷ If you cycle past someone with their hand out for a bus, high-five them.

▷ Even if you don't particularly dislike fit people it's still really good craic to boo joggers in a park.
▷ Be brave.

Mary Nally is another extreme craic merchant in Ireland, originally from the wild west – Galway. 'Defining the craic is an impossible question,' she says. 'The craic is a feeling and is subjective. I think the craic is a little bit magic, created by millions of elements of the right things at the right time. You'll know when you're in it. And I'm pretty sure you can find it on a small island every two years at thing called Drop Everything.'

Nally created Drop Everything, a bi-annual arts and visual festival on Inis Oírr, the smallest of the Aran Islands. It's what inspired Turkfest, the party on Inishturk Island founded by my friend Fionn. 'I wanted to create something I wanted to go to, with art and culture I was interested in, but also solve a problem of over-saturation and this overwhelmed feeling I was experiencing more and more in my day-to-day,' Nally tells me. 'I wanted to pare it back and slow it down. It was really important that there's only one thing on at one time during the event. Inis Oírr, or any island, is an ideal location to test this idea and it helps me to influence change in how an audience experience an event. I want to encourage being present and feeling connected, to each other and also to the planet. Lack of phone coverage and a foggy day can help. An island gives a good sense of place. And being up against, or as I see it, working with the weather is a perfect reminder of how small we are and how not being in control doesn't have to be stressful. It just is. Everyone just needs to calm the fuck down for a minute and remind themselves. So basically if you're at Drop Everything and you're stressed out you're doing it wrong. Come back when you can let go.'

In Ireland, our sense of craic is deeply embedded in booze, particularly pints. I gave up alcohol in the summer of 2013. I had been drinking heavily (as is standard for most Irish women of my generation) for 15 years at that point. For at least five of those years, I had a deep suspicion that my relationship was alcohol was holding me back from reaching my potential as a worker and a person. The craic had actually drained out of drinking for me. The moments of craic paled in comparison to the crippling fear and physical illness of hangovers, especially after I turned 30. I gave it up for three months, only to stay off it, completely teetotal, for four years and counting. I call myself a recovering Irish person.

One of the scariest things about giving up alcohol was, would I be able have the craic without it? Or even scarier, would I be able to *be* the craic without it? The first year or two were all about re-learning how to be the craic in a way that restored rather than depleted my energy reserves. It was tough, I'll admit, but I'm getting to a place where I'm more willing to listen to what I need to do to be happy rather than what others expect of me.

The Sing Along Social encapsulates my approach to restorative craic. It's held in a pub, deliberately on a Sunday night, so it's not necessarily a booze-focused event. Because of the collective power of a bunch of people singing together, it's actually a very effective cure for the fear and because I never put anyone on the spot or make anyone the centre of attention (unless they clearly want to be singled out as a prize winner!), the need for Dutch courage through booze becomes a little redundant.

I still find it hard to be in a social setting without having a job to do, something to keep me busy and active, to help me have the staying power that naturally comes with drinking. So for friends' birthdays I'll take on mini projects like designing customised treasure hunts for them, or I'll cook the food. At weddings, I'll bring the Sing Along Social. At my husband Niall's club night, Lumo, I work on the door. This allows me to participate and be a part of the craic in a way that works for me.

Take a litmus reading of your own craic levels. Have you had the craic recently? Do you need more craic in your life? Who are the craic merchants around you? Give them a call and get craicing.

Here are some ideas for having craic that don't necessarily revolve around alcohol, aren't super expensive and don't take a lot of organisation:

▷ Have a taco party at your house, complete with piñata.
▷ Come to a Sing Along Social (I'll put you on the guestlist!)
▷ Have an old-fashioned sports day with your pals in a public park complete with three-legged races and egg-and-spoon races.

DOING NOTHING

When is the last time you did nothing? When is the last time you stared off into space and day-dreamed? Our smartphones have created a barrier between us and boredom. At the outset this seemed like a positive, but now people are starting to question whether a lack of tolerance for doing nothing is actually good for us.

In the summer of 2017, the American blogger Kristen Hewitt announced that her kids were going to do 'literally nothing' that summer. Instead of cursive writing classes, book projects and summer camp, she decided she was going to allow her daughters to live an unplanned life for a few months and even encourage them to be bored. 'It's so easy to be pressured by things we see on social media. Ways to challenge our kids and enrich their summer,' she wrote on her blog. 'But let's be real – we're all tired. Tired of chores, tired of schedules and places to be, tired of pressure, and tired of unrealistic expectations.'[89] The post went viral.

'I just wanted parents to know that it's OK to not have a Pinterest-perfect summer,' she told the *Huffington Post* in a follow-up interview. 'It's OK to go with the flow and allow your kids to be bored. We have the power to create the life we want, and it's time to start now!'[90]

If you think about the last time you were on a train or a bus, were you looking out of the window, alone with your thoughts? Or were you scrolling on your phone, letting those external influences of other people's updates dictate what you thought about? By not making space for the time to do 'nothing' you could be missing out on crucial day-dreaming time, which will either help you rest your mind or perhaps make space for your next great idea.

Restorative holidays: when you're off, you're off

It is far too easy to justify dipping into your work emails while mid-recovery, and we've already talked about putting up boundaries around technology and your time off. It's different when you're using the technology to help take pressure off, such as a taking a few hours at the desk on a Sunday morning so that you can be fully present at your family lunch on Sunday afternoon. If that's your choice, and it's working for you (and your nearest and dearest), then more power to you.

Catherine Martin has been a Green Party TD for the constituency of Dublin Rathdown since the February 2016 general election. She is deputy leader and education spokesperson for the Green Party. 'I got into politics for my children,' she tells me over the phone from Leinster House. 'My children and my husband are my top priority, followed by my constituents, my party and my country. I joined the Green Party because I was looking to the future, to my children's future.' About a month after being elected, she realised she wasn't seeing enough of her children, her very reason for getting into politics in the first place. Martin and her husband, Francis Duffy, also a Green Party politician and Deputy Mayor at the South Dublin County Council, had to work out a strategic plan that would guarantee, at the very minimum, that at least one of them would be home to tuck their kids into bed every night.

Their children are 10, 9 and 6, and Monday afternoons is Martin's sacred time with them. She tries to keep weekends free, too, but sometimes it's just not possible with party or constituency commitments. What is non-negotiable is a family holiday in the summer. 'We usually go somewhere with hardly any WiFi or phone reception so that I can't be tempted. When I'm off, I'm off.'

'Leinster House is sometimes referred to as a bubble,' Martin tells me. 'It could be a beautiful day outside and you would never see it. Across parties, people offer the advice of "watch out for yourself, watch out for your health and watch out for your family". To be the most effective politician possible, you have to look after your own health. To be the best, you have to feel your best.'

Fallow years

Stefan Sagmeister puts his New York design company, Sagmeister & Walsh, on a year-long sabbatical every seven years. 'I close it for one year to pursue some little experiments which are difficult to accomplish during the regular working year,' explains Sagmeister in a Ted Talk entitled 'The Power of Time Off'. 'In that year, we are not available to any of our clients. We are totally closed. As you can imagine, it's a very lovely and energetic time.'[91]

He had originally opened his studio in New York to combine his two loves of music and design, Sagmeister goes on to say, but he started to see that he and his designers were recycling some of their ideas. That they weren't creating enough newness. That's when he decided to close for a year. He thought it would be helpful to cut off five retirement years at the end of somebody's working life, and intersperse them between the actual working years. 'The work that comes out of these years flows back into the company and the wider society, rather than just benefiting a grandkid or two.'

The idea of taking time off to regenerate is an ancient one. In the same way that many of us have lost touch with the natural elements and phases of the seasons, we seem to have made the mistake of thinking that we have evolved beyond needing a day of rest.

It's time to let go of our guilt around taking time off. Real time off. If we don't take the time off, we won't be able to maintain high performance. Even if we can't take a year off, we should look to the examples above as models of using time off to be better at work. It's our *job* to take time off, or demand it from employers who don't give us enough of it.

FIND THE RIGHT RECOVERY TIME ACTIVITY FOR YOU

So, I'm drawn to crafts, nature, sea swimming, voluntary work and wholesome craic. And I'm working on the art of doing nothing. For you, your recovery time might involve football, a book club, a movie night with pals or mountain climbing.

This is a process of self-awareness. Mindfulness is a skill that has helped me personally in this area. It can help me catch a thought about work and, without giving out to myself, brush it away so that I can regain focus on my chill time. Another skill that has helped is bridging the gap between my Present Self and Future Self, and really, really learning the fact that the yes my Present Self says has a direct impact on the sanity and wellbeing of my Future Self.

Value yourself and your hard work enough to plan for recovery time. Find the activities, and the people, that take you out of your work and replenish rather than drain you. The key for me about time off is respecting that when you're off, you're off. Knowing when to go slow, so that you can have the energy to go fast when you need to, is crucial to our long-term performance.

FIVE SLOW NOTES TO SELF ....

1. Recovery time is part of your job.

▷ Change your perspective on recovery time by accepting that rest is part of your job. If you don't get enough of it, you won't be at your best at work. Don't get into the trap of undervaluing recovery time and therefore letting work seep in to your recovery time.

2. Be strategic about your recovery time.

▷ Plan ahead so that you can build in recovery time after big deadlines or hectic times at work. Remember to introduce your Present Self to your Future Self.

3. Get into crafts, gardening or voluntary work (or whatever takes your mind off work).

▷ Sign up for a creative workshop, a gardening class or give a few hours to a voluntary organisation that you care about. Try something totally different from your work to see if learning a new skill or using your time in a way that's separate from work feels restorative. Alternatively, try doing nothing for short bursts of time and see if being bored suits you.

4. Seek out craic merchants.

▷ Rediscover the restorative nature of good old-fashioned craic. Seek out activities that get you out of your work brain and into a fearless mindset of kicking back and having fun.

5. Think of yourself as a human version of Glastonbury Festival.

▷ Even if you can't take a fallow year, you should at least take a fallow weekend or a fallow hour to help your recovery time, so that you can come back to work fresher than ever.

SLOW READS (MY CURRENT FAVOURITE BEACH BOOKS) ....

- *I Found My Tribe* by Ruth Fitzmaurice

- *Love in Row 27* by Eithne Shortall

- *Oh My God, What a Complete Aisling* by Emer McLysaght and Sarah Breen

Slow Burners

It turns out you *can* slow down and keep up. It just depends on what your idea of keeping up is.

So, did I really slow down at work? Two years after my epiphany, I actually seemed to be 'busier' than ever. My various projects were thriving and new opportunities continued to present themselves. But *I* was a little different; the internal pace of my experience had become a calmer place to be because of the lessons I learned along the way.

Here's a handy list of the ten most important things I learned when writing this book. You know, just in case you didn't quite have the time to read the whole thing. It's OK. I know you're busy.

Ten slow burners

1.   It's essential to know the difference between procrastination and percolation. Are you avoiding something because you're afraid of failure or do your

ideas need a little more time to bake before they're ready to be served? If you are indeed procrastinating, it helps to focus on the *process* and not the *result*. Introduce your Present Self to your Future Self. You guys have *got* to start getting along.

2. Getting to know your Inner Critic, and even giving them a name (like my Aunt Linda) can help you notice when they're in the room. It might help you to figure out how to work with them rather than fighting against them.

3. Embrace the fact that you have three brains (your head, your heart and your gut) and learn how to get them to start working together. This can be particularly useful in learning how to harness the power of no. Investigate working with a life coach or use a toolkit like *mBraining* to learn more about how to get your three brains to communicate with each other.[92]

4. Self-awareness is key when working with others. Investing in working with a life coach or, if you want to go deeper, a talk therapist, will pay off in the long run.

5. Accept, *really* accept, that busyness is not necessarily a sign of success, efficiency or productivity. Learn the difference between true and false urgency. Don't let work

be the framework that your life squeezes into; your life should be the framework that work fits into.

6. You can save money, and therefore loosen the grip of golden handcuffs, by indulging in a little slow, conscientious shopping. Don't fall into the trap of fast shopping and compulsive spending.

7. Try to avoid chain-scrolling on your smartphone, and take time to re-evaluate how you use your technology. If you're not into traditional alarm clocks, put your phone on airplane mode when it's in your bedroom. You definitely don't need to check your emails last thing at night and first thing in the morning.

8. Learn how to manage your energy as well as your time, by eating, sleeping and exercising well, and by paying attention to how your own personal energy cycle flows. Figure out what you need to feel well and develop healthy habits around diet, sleep and exercise that support your wellbeing.

9. If you are sensitive to the distractions of stuff, sounds and smells, curating your office environment in a way that works for you will help you cultivate a slower, calmer and ultimately more productive work space.

10. Recovery time is a part of your job. It is a non-negotiable aspect of your work that needs to be scheduled in and respected. Taking breaks during your work day and taking proper time off at the weekend and on holidays is essential to maintaining high performance at work. Perhaps the most important skill to learn is when to go fast, and when to go slow.

These are the key lessons I learned and then forgot, and then had to learn again, all in the process of researching and writing this book. It turns out changing your approach to work takes practice. It will take an investment in time. You'll need to figure out what *your* good life is and what you need to change to make it a reality. As Tony Crabbe writes in *Busy: How To Thrive In a World of Too Much*, 'You're busy because you haven't made tough choices and asserted your will on your environment. Mastering a world of too much involves the ability to make deliberate and intentional choices.'

I haven't quite mastered the art of 'slow at work' just yet. Even though I wrote a whole book on how to slow down at work, complete with clear solutions and exit points from the cult of busyness, as I approached the end of the project I felt a little burnt out, to be honest. But writing this book has been a life-changing challenge. It has helped me to shine a light on some of the unhealthy patterns I have created around work. It gave me the opportunity to figure out a set of boundaries and a framework around which to build a slower, more sustainable approach to work.

It has also reminded me that change is a long, constant process. It's the ultimate slow work.

I used to find it so frustrating that I couldn't just change *now*. That I couldn't just erase my history, my genetic make-up and my learned behaviour in an instant. Why couldn't I learn how to work slowly, like, really quickly?

One evening recently my sea-swimming pal Oonagh and I were on the way home from a cold summer swim when our chat turned to the subject of change and how circular it is. Oonagh drew a sketch in her notebook of these interacting circles of change. We keep coming around to the same lessons over and over again, until the change finally sinks in.

Personal change takes *ages*. But when you feel like you are on the way to becoming a different person, when you get little signs that you're listening to yourself, or that you're motivated not by praise from others but by an inner compass, or you notice that your Inner Critic's voice has softened somewhat ... then those circles of change become an exciting place to be.

Let it go

'There was a time, in the not so distant past, when "being on top of things" was not only realistic, but expected. Those days are gone. We have to let go of our fantasy of getting back in control through better organisation; there is just too much information and too many demands on us,' writes Tony Crabbe in *Busy: How to Thrive in A World Of Too Much*. 'Buffeted by wave after wave of demands, we become overwhelmed, defeated and even begin to feel guilty. Accept it; you will never, ever be in control of everything again.'

That should be hard for a recovering control freak to hear, but for me it's actually quite a relief. Letting go has been a continuous thread through the talks I've had about this book project.

'Pulling yourself out of burnout is about embracing your own capacity,' Annika Fogarty of Mind Smart says. Embracing your own capacity. That to me hits the nail on the head of burnout and banana-level busyness.

You are probably a very capable person. But you have limitations. And that's OK. That's normal. We are not all Beyoncé. Even Beyoncé probably isn't 'Beyoncé'. If you can embrace and accept your own capacity, if you can lower your expectations (in a good way), it can take an awful lot of that pressure off you. For me, that release of pressure is where the magic of slow lies.

What can you take out of your life that is making you feel too stretched? Do you really have to make all the cupcakes for the parent–teacher meeting at the school again? Or can someone else do it this time? Or can you buy them in your local bakery? Do you absolutely have to work over the weekend to reach a Monday morning deadline or can you ask for more time, so that you can take a proper break and hit the ground running at the start of the new week? Do you really want to take on this project or are you just saying yes so as not to disappoint others?

Burnout and busyness are relative. But we have become competitive about our busyness, haven't we? Take an honest look at how you feel when you send an email close to midnight or at dawn, or when you cancel another meet-up with a friend in favour of staying late at the office. Are you being a work martyr? Is that who you really want to be? Can you take a step out of the cult of busyness and forge a path at your own pace?

I think you can. There may be consequences. Maybe you won't get a promotion. Maybe you'll need to accept that you've reached the peak of your pay grade. Maybe you'll have to embrace the power of no, and pass on opportunities.

What is more important to you, *really*? Your health and happiness? Or your work and money? I'm not here to judge what your answer is. But I'm here to ask you this: what are the costs of burnout versus the gains of working all day, every day, without prioritising recovery time? Are you choosing work or life?

'In the workplace,' Carl Honoré, author of *In Praise of Slow* tells me, 'those who will inherit the earth are those who know what speed to do things at. They know that certain things are fast, while other things need slowness. It's about the dance between the two. The magic happens in that music as you move back and forth between fast and slow.'

For me, slow means calm and considered yet flexible, fluid and loosely controlled – anything too rigid feels like the enemy of slow. It definitely doesn't mean coming to a complete stop. Instead, it's about stepping outside the cult of busyness to gain some perspective on the way we are choosing to spend our work days and whether we have the power to change that to make it more sustainable. Personally, I feel much clearer about what choice I want to make. I'm choosing my health and happiness. I'm leaving the cult of busyness.

It turns out that the secret of slow work is giving ourselves the space and time we need to master the art of knowing when to go fast and when to go slow.

Thank Yous

When I first started this project, I was all set to embark on a marathon. Pretty soon down the road, however, I realised writing a book was more like a triathlon. And then finally it dawned on me – I was on a decathlon, and I wasn't even wearing the right shoes. There were so many people along the road of *Slow at Work* who cheered me on, encouraged me not to give up and inspired me to keep going. I'm so very grateful to all of them.

The insights of everyone I interviewed for *Slow at Work* and for the slow:series workshops has informed the book that you now hold in your hands. Thank you so much to Alan Lyons, Alicia Byrne, Andrew Hyland, Anne-Marie Downey, Annika Fogarty, Aoibheann McNamara, Austin Hogan, Áine, Billy Byrne, Blindboy Boatclub, Carl Honoré, Catherine Martin TD, Ciaran Hogan, Clare Grennan, Clare Mulvany, Cliodhna Prendergast, Colin Harmon, Darina Allen, Dave Dunne, Dave Smith, David Ferguson, David Prior, Deirdre McSwiney, Derval O'Rourke, Donal Skehan, Dr Colin O'Driscoll, Dr Harry Barry, Dr Iseult Freeney, Dr John Cryan, Dr Stephen Kinsella, Duggy, Eithne Shortall, Emily Bereskin, Emily Robyn Archer,

Emma Norton, Elsa Jones, Fiona Brennan, Fiona Cribben, Hans & Gaby Wieland, Henry Seward, Imen McDonnell, Irene Patel, James Kavanagh, Jamia Wilson, Jenny Blake, Johanna Fullerton, John Graham, Josephine Lynch, Kathy Scott, Kevin Thornton, Kim Keating, Laura Caffrey, Leisha McGrath, Lisa O'Neill, Lizzie Fitzpatrick, Mari Kennedy, Mark Boyle, Mary Catherine Heanue, Helen Heanue, Philomena Heaney and all my friend on Inishturk Island, Mary Nally, Melrona Kirrane, Michael Kelly, Michelle Darmody, Muriel Thornton, Nathalie Marquez Courtney, Niall Crumlish, Oonagh Murphy, Paul Brennan, Racheal O'Mara, Richard McDonnell, Rob Farhat, Robbie McDonald and the Tyrone Guthrie Centre, Roisín Agnew, Ronan Hession, Ruairí McKiernan, Sallay Matu Garnett, Sally Foran, Sam McNicholl, Sarah Butler, Sarah Reynolds, Shamash Aladina, Sharon Greene, Simon Cohen, Simon Roche, Sister Pauline McGaley, Stephen O'Reilly, Steve McCarthy, Angela and Margaret Dorgan, Sorca McGrath, Tess Brady, the Venerable Panchen Ötrul Rinpoche and Triona Lillis. An especially enormous thank you to Aisling Rogerson and Luca D'Alfonso at The Fumbally for their support and exemplification of the idea of *Slow at Work* from the very beginning.

I'd like to thank the team at Gill Books for holding my hand throughout the process and being firm but fair cheerleaders along the way. I'd particularly like to thank my Commissioning Editor Sarah Liddy for having faith in my idea from the word go and my Managing Editor Catherine Gough for getting me across the finish line.

To everyone I've ever worked with, thank you for everything you've taught me. A special mention must go to Aoife Flynn who showed me by her example that it was possible to be slow (and still very, very good) at work. To my editors Laurence Mackin and Rachel Collins at *The Irish Times* for their support of my scribbles and their patience in the face of my procrastinating ways.

Thank you to my therapist, Emma, who has so skilfully helped me unpack and examine my relationship to work and praise. To my dear and ever-patient friends, particularly Fionn Kidney, Kristin Jensen, Conor Wilson and Anna Jacob, who have been such compassionate listeners throughout the evolution of *Slow at Work*, thank you.

A special thanks to my beloved sister Niamh McElwain who meticulously corrected all of the early drafts of *Slow at Work*, and who knew exactly how to offer up the kind of encouraging feedback that even Aunt Linda could take on board without having a mini meltdown. I'd like to thank my family, the

McElwains and the Byrnes, for their encouragement and unwavering belief in me.

Thanks to my dog Daffodil for being the best percolation partner on the planet. The most effusive of thank yous are directed to my husband, Niall Byrne. Thank you for being my relentless champion, an unstoppable ledgebag, and an all-round good guy.

NOTES

1   Jon Weiner, 'WPO Global Population Analysis Summary',
    http://www.workplaceoptions.com/wp-content/
    uploads/2015/12/WPO-Global-Population-Analysis-
    Summary.pdf, 17 December 2015

2   Alison Coleman, 'Over half of UK workers have
    experienced "burnout" in their job', virgin.com, https://
    www.virgin.com/disruptors/over-half-uk-workers-have-
    experienced-burnout-their-job, 15 April 2015

3   Blánaid Hayes, 'The National Study of Wellbeing of
    Hospital Doctors in Ireland', rcpi.com, https://www.rcpi.
    ie/research/hospital-doctors-wellbeing, 2014

4   Emma Seppala and Marissa King, 'Burnout at Work Isn't
    Just About Exhaustion. It's Also About Loneliness', hbr.org,
    https://hbr.org/2017/06/burnout-at-work-isnt-just-about-
    exhaustion-its-also-about-loneliness,29 June 2017

5   Patrick Freyne, *Burnt out? Relax, we've been exhausted
    for centuries,* Irishtimes.com, https://www.irishtimes.
    com/life-and-style/health-family/burnt-out-relax-we-ve-
    been-exhausted-for-centuries-1.3213153, 16 September
    2017

6   James Sherk, *Upwards Leisure Mobility: Americans Work Less and Have More Leisure Time*, Heritage.org, http://www.heritage.org/jobs-and-labor/report/upwards-leisure-mobility-americans-work-less-and-have-more-leisuretime-ever, 31 August 2007

7   Amy X Wang, *We're Not Actually That Busy But We're Great At Pretending We Are*, qz.com, https://qz.com/499575/were-not-actually-that-busy-but-were-great-at-pretending-we-are, 11 September 2015

8   Margaret Atwood, twitter.com, https://twitter.com/margaretatwood/status/431142446852878338, 5 February 2014

9   Douglas Adams, *The Salmon of Doubt*, Basingstoke: Macmillan, 2002

10   Tim Urban, 'Why Procrastinators Procrastinate', waitbutwhy.com, https://waitbutwhy.com/2013/10/why-procrastinators-procrastinate.html, 30 October 2013

11   Daniel Kahneman, *Thinking, Fast and Slow*, New York: Farrar, Straus and Giroux, 2011

12   Jane Burka and Lenora Yuen, *Procrastination: Why You Do It, What To Do About It*, 2nd Edn, Boston: De Capo Lifelong Book, 2008 (1st Edn 1983)

13   Carol S Dweck, *Mindset: The New Psychology of Success*, New York: Ballantine Books, 2006

14 School of Life, 'Carol Dweck on Perfectionism',
    theschooloflife.com, https://www.youtube.com/
    watch?v=XgUF5WalyDk, July 2013

15 John Perry, *The Art of Procrastination: A Guide to
    Effective Dawdling, Lollygagging and Postponing*, New
    York: Workman Publishing Company, 2012

16 Stephen Guise, *How To Be An Imperfectionist: The
    New Way to Self-Acceptance, Fearless Living, and
    Freedom from Perfectionism*, Columbus, OH: Selective
    Entertainment LLC, 2015

17 Richard Branson, 'Why I Wake Up Early', virgin.com,
    https://www.virgin.com/richard-branson/why-i-wake-
    early, 2 October 2014

18 Anne Lamott, *Bird by Bird: Some Instructions on Writing
    and Life*, New York: Anchor, 1995

19 Nicholas Carlson, 'The "Dirty Little Secret" About
    Google's 20% Time, According To Marissa Mayer',
    uk.businessinsider.com, http://uk.businessinsider.
    com/mayer-google-20-time-does-not-exist-2015-
    1?r=US&IR=T, 13 January 2015

20 Hal and Sirda Stone, *Embracing Your Inner Critic: Turning
    Self-Criticism Into A Creative Asset*, San Francisco: Harper
    One, 1993

21 Sarah Green Carmichael, 'Make Peace With Your Inner Critic', hbr.org, https://hbr.org/ideacast/2016/01/make-peace-with-your-inner-critic.html, 14 January 2016

22 Rick Hanson, 'Confronting The Negativity Bias', rickhanson.com, http://www.rickhanson.net/how-your-brain-makes-you-easily-intimidated/, 26 October 2010

23 Pauline Rose Clance and Suzanne Imes, 'The Imposter Phenomenon in High Achieving Women: Dynamics and Therapeutic Intervention', *Psychotherapy Theory, Research and Practice*, Vol. 15 no. 3, Fall 1978

24 Amy Cuddy, *Presence: Bringing Your Boldest Self To Your Biggest Challenges*, Boston: Little, Brown & Company, 2015

25 John Gravois, 'You're Not Fooling Anyone', chronicle.com, http://www.chronicle.com/article/Youre-Not-Fooling-Anyone/28069, 9 November 2007

26 Natalie Portman, 'Natalie Portman Harvard Commencement Speech', https://www.youtube.com/watch?v=jDaZu_KEMCY, 27 May 2015

27 White House Press Office, *2010 Annual Report To Congress on White House Staff*, obamawhitehouse.archives.gov, https://obamawhitehouse.archives.gov/briefing-room/disclosures/annual-records/2010, 2010

28   Tom Murse, 'Michelle Obama's Staff', thoughtco. com, https://www.thoughtco.com/michelle-obamas-staff-3322113, 6 May 2017

29   Amy Poehler, *Yes Please*, New York: HarperCollins, 2014

30   Barry Schwartz, *The Paradox of Choice: Why More Is Less?*, New York: Harper Perennial, 2004; 'The Paradox of Choice', ted.com, https://www.ted.com/talks/barry_schwartz_on_the_paradox_of_choice, July 2005

31   Folio, 'Don't Give In To Imposter Syndrome', folio.ca, http://www.folio.ca/dont-give-in-to-impostor-syndrome-astrophysics-pioneer-tells-grads, 14 June 2016

32   Marvin Oka and Grant Soosalu, *mBraining: Using Your Multiple Brains to do Cool Stuff*, CreateSpace Independent Publishing Platform, 2012

33   Lindsay Dodgson, 'This CEO's Absolutely Perfect Response to Someone Taking a Day Off for Mental Health is a Master Class in Leadership', inc.com, https://www.inc.com/business-insider/madalyn-parker-ben-congleton-olark-live-chat-lesson-leadership.html, 11 July 2017

34   Steven R Covey, *The 7 Habits of Highly Effective People*, New York: Free Press, 1989

35   Anne Loehr, 'How To Live With Purpose, Identify Your Values and Improve Your Leadership', huffingtonpost. com, http://www.huffingtonpost.com/anne-loehr/how-to-live-with-purpose-_b_5187572.html, 6 May 2014

36   Gretchen Rubin, *The Happiness Project: Or, Why I Spent a Year Trying to Sing in the Morning, Clean My Closets, Fight Right, Read Aristotle, and Generally Have More Fun*, New York: Harper Paperbacks, 2009

37   Peter F Drucker, *Managing Oneself*, Cambridge, MA: Harvard Business Press, 2008

38   David D Burns, *Feeling Good: The New Mood Therapy*, New York: William Morrow & Company, 1980

39   Alfie Kohn, *Punished by Rewards: The Trouble with Gold Stars, Incentive Plans, As, Praise and Other Bribes*, 2nd Edn, Boston: Mariner Books, 1999

40   Anthony K Tjan, '5 Ways To Become Self-Aware', hbr.org, https://hbr.org/2015/02/5-ways-to-become-more-self-aware, 11 February 2015

41   Carl Rogers, *On Becoming a Person: A Therapist's View of Psychotherapy*, Boston: Mariner Books, 1961

42   Dan Goldstein, 'The Battle Between Your Present and Future Self', ted.com, https://www.ted.com/talks/daniel_goldstein_the_battle_between_your_present_and_future_self, November 2011

43   Dan Gilbert, 'The Psychology of Your Future Self', ted.com, https://www.ted.com/talks/dan_gilbert_you_are_always_changing, March 2014

44   Daniel M Bartels and Oleg Urminsky, 'On Intertemporal Selfishness: How the Perceived Instability of Identity

Underlies Impatient Consumption', Chicago: *Journal of Consumer Research*, August 2011. Further information: ejcr.org

45   Priyanka D Joshi and Nathanael J Fast, 'Power and Reduced Temporal Discounting', sagepub. com, http://journals.sagepub.com/doi/ abs/10.1177/0956797612457950, 12 February 2013

46   René Redzepi, 'Culture of The Kitchen', Madfeed.co, https://www.madfeed.co/2015/culture-of-the-kitchen-rene-redzepi/,12 August 2015

47   John Kroenig, 'Sonder: The Realization That Everyone Has a Story', https://www.youtube.com/ watch?v=AkoML0_FiV4, 26 October 2014

48   Kronos Incorporated and Future Workplace, 'The Employee Burnout Crisis: Study Reveals Big Workplace Challenge in 2017', kronos.com, https://www.kronos. com/about-us/newsroom/employee-burnout-crisis-study-reveals-big-workplace-challenge-2017, 9 January 2017

49   Roisín Agnew, 'Feeling The Burnout: Is The Modern Working Model Broken?', image.ie, http://www.image.ie/ life/article/feeling-the-burnout-is-the-modern-working-model-broken/, 18 July 2017

50   Barbara Ehrenreich, 'Hers', nytimes.com, http://www. nytimes.com/1985/02/21/garden/hers.html, 21 February 1985

51 Daniel J Levitin, *The Organized Mind: Thinking Straight In The Age of Information Overload*, New York: Dutton, 2015

52 Tony Crabbe, *Busy: How to Thrive in a World of Too Much*, New York: Grand Central Publishing, 2015

53 Project: Time Off, 'The Work Martyr's Cautionary Tale', https://www.projecttimeoff.com/research/work-martyrs-cautionary-tale, 2016

54 Claire McCormack, 'Why Farmer Burnout Could Derail Dairy Sector Growth (90 hour working weeks not unusual)', independent.ie, http://www.independent.ie/business/farming/dairy/why-farmer-burnout-could-derail-dairy-sector-growth-90hour-working-weeks-not-unusual-35629781.html, 18 April 2017

55 Martin Ryan, 'Dairy Farms The Most Lethal Workplace', independent.ie http://www.independent.ie/business/farming/dairy-farms-the-most-lethal-workplace-hsa-34518915.html, March 8 2016

56 Bertrand Russell, *In Praise of Idleness*, Didcot: Routledge, 1935

57 Julie Clow, *The Work Revolution: Freedom and Excellence For All*, Hoboken, NJ: Wiley, 2012

58 Shamash Alidina, 'The Mindful Way Through Stress', https://www.youtube.com/watch?v=ouQSPAzSLzQ, 26 November 2012

59 Colin Gleeson, 'Rents Dwarf Celtic Tiger era with "disastrous effect" on society', irishtimes.com, https://www.irishtimes.com/business/personal-finance/rents-dwarf-celtic-tiger-era-with-disastrous-effect-on-society-1.2857722, 8 November 2016

60 Pobal, 'Early Years Sector Profile 2015–2016', pobal.ie, https://www.pobal.ie/Publications/Documents/Latest%20Early%20Years%20Sector%20Profile%20Published.pdf, 2016

61 Mark Boyle, *The Moneyless Man: A Year of Freeconomic Living*, London: Oneworld, 2010

62 Miles Brignall, 'The Moneyless Man who gave up on cash and embraced foraging and farming', guardian.com, https://www.theguardian.com/money/2015/sep/04/moneyless-man-gave-up-cash-embraced-foraging-farming, 4 September 2015

63 Daniel Kahneman and Angus Deaton, 'High income improves evaluation of life but not emotional well-being', princeton.edu, https://www.princeton.edu/~deaton/downloads/deaton_kahneman_high_income_improves_evaluation_August2010.pdf, 4 July 2010

64 Paul Keegan, 'Gravity Payments' Dan Price Wins Court Battle With His Brother', inc.com, https://www.inc.com/paul-keegan/dan-price-gravity-lawsuit-win.html, 8 July 2016

65 Ethan Wolff-Man, 'What the new Nobel Prize Winner has to say about money and happiness', time.com, http://time.com/money/4070041/angus-deaton-nobel-winner-money-happiness/, 13 October 2015

66 Pippa Stephens, 'Boss of £1m firm will give it away to be a full-time dad', http://www.bbc.com/news/business-26717509, 24 March 2014

67 Abraham H Maslow, 'A Theory of Human Motivation', *Psychological Review* Vol. 50 no. 4, 1943

68 Catherine Cleary, 'Supermarket vs Local Market', irishtimes.com, https://www.irishtimes.com/life-and-style/food-and-drink/supermarket-vs-local-market-1.1794710, 18 May 2014

69 NPR, 'Interview with Charlie Brooker by Terry Gross', npr.org, http://www.npr.org/2016/10/20/498683379/black-mirror-creator-dramatizes-our-worst-nightmares-about-technology, 20 October 2016

70 Camp Grounded: Supper Camp for Adults, http://campgrounded.org/

71 Jocelyn K Glei, *Unsubscribe: How To Kill Email Anxiety, Avoid Distractions and Get Real Work Done*, New York: PublicAffairs, 2016

72 Tony Crabbe, *Busy: How to Thrive in a World of Too Much*, New York: Grand Central Publishing, 2015

73   Adrienne LaFrance, 'The Triumph of Email: Why does one of the world's most reviled technologies keep winning?', https://www.theatlantic.com/technology/archive/2016/01/what-comes-after-email/422625/, 6 January 2016

74   Cal Newport, *Deep Work: Rules for Focused Success in a Distracted World*, London: Piatkus, 2016

75   Catherine Blyth, *On Time: Finding Your Pace in a World Addicted To Fast*, London: HarperCollins, 2017

76   Tony Schwartz, 'The Productivity Paradox: How Sony Pictures Gets More Out of People by Demanding Less', hbr.org, https://hbr.org/2010/06/the-productivity-paradox-how-sony-pictures-gets-more-out-of-people-by-demanding-less, June 2010

77   Ron Friedman, 'What You Eat Affects Your Productivity', hbr.org, https://hbr.org/2014/10/what-you-eat-affects-your-productivity, 17 October 2014

78   John Cryan, 'Feed Your Microbes: Nurture Your Mind', https://www.youtube.com/watch?v=vKxomLM7SVc, 11 July 2017

79   Marcello Solinas and others, 'Caffeine Induces Dopamine and Glutamate Release in the Shell of the Nucleus Accumbens', *Journal of Neuroscience* 22 (15), http://www.jneurosci.org/content/22/15/6321.short, August 2002

80 Meghan Lodwick, 'Caffeine the hallucinogen', latrobe.
    edu.au, https://www.latrobe.edu.au/news/articles/2011/
    article/caffeine-is-the-most-commonly-used-drug, 2011

81 Michael Childs, 'UGA kinesiology researchers find single
    bout of exercise boosts energy', news.uga.edu, http://
    news.uga.edu/releases/article/uga-kinesiology-exercise-
    boosts-energy/, 3 December 2013

82 Charles Duhigg, *The Power Of Habit: Why We Do What
    We Do in Life and Business*, New York: Random House,
    2013

83 Roisín Ingle, 'How Ruth Fitzmaurice found her tribe
    in Ladies' Cove in Greystones', irishtimes.com,
    https://www.irishtimes.com/life-and-style/people/
    how-ruth-fitzmaurice-found-her-tribe-in-ladies-cove-
    greystones-1.3128069, 1 July 2017

84 BBC, 'Is Hot Desking All Good?', bbc.co.uk, http://www.
    bbc.co.uk/guides/zgjmtfr, 2014

85 University of Wolverhampton, 'Taking The Hot Desk',
    wlv.co.uk, https://www.wlv.ac.uk/about-us/news-and-
    events/wlvdialogue/previous-issues/wlvdialogue---
    summer-2011/taking-the-hot-desk/, 2011

86 Craig Knight and Alex Haslam, 'The relative merits of
    lean, enriched and empowered offices: an experimental
    examination of the impact of workspace management
    strategies on well-being and productivity', https://

www.ncbi.nlm.nih.gov/pubmed/20565201, *Journal of Experimental Psychology: Applied* 16 (2), June 2010

87   Diane Hoskins, 'Employees Perform Better When They Can Control Their Space', hbr.org, https://hbr.org/2014/01/employees-perform-better-when-they-can-control-their-space, 16 January 2014

88   Carl Honoré, *In Praise of Slow: How a Worldwide Movement Is Challenging The Cult of Speed*, Toronto: Vintage Canada, 2004

89   Kristin Hewitt, 'Why We Are Doing Nothing This Summer', kristenhewitt.me, http://kristenhewitt.me/why-we-are-doing-nothing-this-summer-2/, June 2017

90   Caroline Bologna, 'Mom declares her kids are doing "literally nothing" this summer in viral post', huffingtonpost.com, http://www.huffingtonpost.com/entry/mom-declares-her-kids-are-doing-literally-nothing-this-summer-in-viral-post_us_594d4066e4b0da2c731b37fe, 23 June 2017

91   Stephen Sagmeister, 'The Power of Time Off', ted.com, https://www.ted.com/talks/stefan_sagmeister_the_power_of_time_off, July 2009

92   Marvin Oka and Grant Soosalu, *mBraining: Using Your Multiple Brains to do Cool Stuff*, CreateSpace Independent Publishing Platform, 2012